WOMAN UP!

FINDING EQUALITY

STORIES
OF AMERICAN WOMEN

Linda Hanson, Ed.D.

NEWMAN SPRINGS PUBLISHING
320 Broad Street
Red Bank, NJ 07701

First originally published by Newman Springs Publishing 2022

Disclaimer
The information provided in this book is for educational
or general purposes. This book is accurate to the best
of the author's knowledge, and the author disclaims
any liability in connection with the information.

ISBN 978-1-68498-268-4 (Paperback)
ISBN 978-1-68498-269-1 (Digital)

Printed in the United States of America

CONTENTS

Acknowledgments v
Introduction..vii

Chapter 1: Language Defines Us....................................1
Chapter 2: Professional Women 16
Chapter 3: Formative Years 37
Chapter 4: A Turn for Women 59
Chapter 5: The Science of Being a Woman.................74
Chapter 6: Our Feminist Foremothers 95
Chapter 7: Women Warriors...107
Chapter 8: Rowing through Waves...............................115
Chapter 9: Anti-Feminism 129
Chapter 10: And Justice for All......................................145

ACKNOWLEDGMENTS

Thank you to Bob Hanson, Lynne Madden, and Linnea Nelson for support and encouragement.

INTRODUCTION

Women grow radical with age. One day an army of gray-haired women may quietly take over the earth.

—Gloria Steinem

Full disclosure: I saw the Beatles debut on *The Ed Sullivan Show*. I have witnessed women looking for fairness in structures, norms, and rules for three quarters of a century. When I stretch my conceptual arms to either side of my life, I touch three centuries of women. My grandmother was born in the nineteenth century, my daughters in the twentieth century, and my granddaughters in the twenty-first century, who, with today's life expectancy, may live into the twenty-second century. *Woman Up!* recounts stories of generations of women across time. Each era witnesses challenges and defeats as well as triumphs of positive change. *Woman Up!* explores the journey of women in the United States through the centuries who have demanded equality (equal opportunities and resources) and equity (opportunities and resources needed for each person to reach equal outcomes). *Woman Up!* examines the relationships between women and language, societal norms, science, careers, legislative decisions, femicide, violence, eugenics, feminism, and other compelling topics.

Why now? Haven't we resolved the issues of gender inequality? Not yet. According to the Bureau of Labor Statistics, women represented 100 percent of the jobs lost in December 2020.[1] One-fourth of women say they are financially worse off in 2021 than they were

---

[1] "The Employment Situation," *Bureau of Labor Statistics*, January 8, 2021, https://www.bls.gov/news.release/archives/empsit_02052021.pdf.

the previous year.[2] Maternal mortality with preterm birth rates is rising for the fifth year in a row and is getting worse.[3] According to the most recent complete information available from the National Cancer Institute's SEER database, the five-year survival rate has increased in ten of eleven common cancers from 1975 to 2013. The survival rate of prostate cancer has increased from 66.3 percent in 1975 to 98 percent in 2013.

The single cancer that has lost progress is uterine cancer. Uterine cancer has declined from an 88 percent survival rate in 1975 to 82.5 percent in 2013. Research in this area receives the least funding of any of the eleven common cancers. The Supreme Court of the United States undermined *Roe v. Wade* in a 2021 ruling. Women have moved backward to a time when women had few rights to make decisions about their bodies. Women still face harassment and bias in the workplace, experience wage gaps compared to men, and bear most of the responsibility for balancing family and job duties. They are the fastest-growing group in US prisons.

The word *feminism* does not have a male equivalent word because over centuries, men created the systems, rules, and norms that ensured their supremacy. Feminism is a backlash to the inherent, one-sided path that men designed for women to walk down. Women are at a pivotal point in the narration of their own stories. Understanding the past, the present, and the desired future will help us know what we stand for and who stands with us. We are charged to forge a path of equality and equity moving forward. Women are still in a quest for fairness. Our future has yet to be chronicled.

---

[2] Heather Long and Emily Gusion, "A quarter of women say they are financially worse off a year into pandemic, Post-ABC poll finds," *The Washington Post*, April 2, 2021, https://www.washingtonpost.com/business/2021/04/27/poll-women-pandemic-worse-off/.

[3] Emily Laurence, "New Data Shows Maternal and Infant Mortality Rates in the US Are Getting Worse—Here's What Needs to Change," *Well and Good*, November 16, 2020, https://www.wellandgood.com/march-dimes-report-card/.

CHAPTER 1

Language Defines Us

Our attitudes about language and culture and people flow
through each other without us realizing the equivalency.
—Rebecca Wheeler, 2019

In prepandemic times, I attended a gathering of active and retired female public school superintendents who were discussing tough educational issues. A woman complimented her colleague's courage by saying, "That took balls."

First, I am sure this particular woman did not have balls, and second, balls just hang and then disappear at the first hint of danger, so why do balls denote courage? I helpfully added, "That *was* courageous. That took a vagina!"

Everyone looked at me with astonishment. I explained, vaginas, not balls, should be synonymous with courage. Ten-pound babies push through this four-inch orifice. That takes vaginal courage! Women have populated the earth through months of discomfort, morning sickness, carrying a bowling ball on their bladders, followed by excruciatingly painful births, recovery with stitches, oozing breast milk, and sometimes profound depression. At the end of this process, we call the result mankind. Is this our reward for pushing out 7.55 billion people who populate the earth today? As we female superintendents meditated on these matters, we munched popcorn while pushing aside the "old maids" in the bowl—those kernels that haven't been popped.

Language about women has been studied by writers, psychologists, sociologists, researchers, and linguists. The impact of language on societal norms has long been an area of interest for people who believe that individual words provide the foundation for unconscious bias. Although there is disagreement whether denigrating language perpetuates sexist conditions, everyday observations reveal how men use unflattering language about women. Surprisingly, many women use the same language about themselves. Other women remain silent when they hear language that demeans them. Are women thick-skinned, obtuse, complicit, or do they not want to wade into the waters of confrontation?

Rebecca Wheeler, professor of linguistics at Christopher Newport University, says, "Linguists say, as we see a people, so we see their language; as we see a language, so we see its people."[4] Language is at the heart of how we shape perceptions and understand groups of people. Words matter.

While a public school superintendent, I was asked to give a presentation for aspiring female superintendents, which I titled The Feng Shui of Finance. I wondered why any speech that benefited aspiring female superintendents would not equally benefit aspiring male superintendents. However, my assignment was to speak to an audience of women. I decided to experiment by using "women's language" throughout the presentation.

As I prepared, I discovered that almost all leadership language is the language of men. I found a few old-fashioned women's metaphors: stick to your knitting, too many cooks in the kitchen, or a watched pot never boils—all of which stem from home and hearth. I realized that women do not share an equivalent vocabulary set when it comes to leadership. Instead, leadership language—developed by men, about men, and used by all—was easy to reference. The dearth

---

4   Michael Hobbs, "Why America Needs Ebonics Now," *HuffPost*, September 25, 2017, https://highline.huffingtonpost.com/articles/en/ebonics/.

of women's leadership language caused me to dig deeper into the history and thinking about language and its impact on women.

While the language and attitudes *about* women have been studied, language used *by* women has not been an equal area of interest. Men have used laws, science, and society's censure to keep women in their homes and in their places. In many cases, women have embraced those strictures, not even questioning if there could be another possibility. Men have been obstacles in the lives of women, but so have women.

In this decade, our country has been conflicted about gender equality. According to a Pew Research Center report from 2017, 66 percent of men and women in both political parties believe that recent sexual harassment allegations primarily reflect widespread societal problems. About six in ten women and four in ten men state the country has not gone far enough when it comes to gender equality.[5]

Abodo, an organization that conducts research about various living conditions, stated no group is more hated than women when it comes to online prejudice. One study reviewed twelve million tweets sent from June 2014 to December 2015 and produced US maps that illustrated derogatory language against women. The search terms *cunt*, *twat*, *hag*, and *bitch* resulted in the state of Louisiana's having the most sexist tweets with 894 per one hundred thousand. New Orleans took first prize as a city with 3,696 sexist language tweets per one hundred thousand tweets with Atlanta coming in second with 1,580 per one hundred thousand. The states that used the most discriminatory language against women tended to be in the southeast.[6]

---

[5] "On Gender Differences, No Consensus on Nature vs. Nurture," *Pew Research Center*, December 5, 2017, https://www.pewresearch.org/social-trends/2017/12/05/on-gender-differences-no-consensus-on-nature-vs-nurture/.

[6] Christina Cauterucci, "Louisiana Wins Title of State With the Most Prejudice Tweets," Slate.com, March 8, 2016, https://slate.com/human-interest/2016/03/the-states-with-the-highest-concentrations-of-racist-misogynist-and-homophobic-tweets.html.

Walt Wolfram sums up the impact of language on our thinking about how we view groups of people:

> It's easy to figure out which dialects are most desirable and which dialects are less desirable, just look at which groups are more desirable and which groups are less desirable. We tend to think of urban as better than rural. We tend to think of middle class as better than working class. We tend to think of White as better than Black, so if you're a member of one of these stigmatized groups, then the way you talk will also be stigmatized.[7]

Ebonics

Stigmatized language became the center of a heated debate at the end of the twentieth century. The wide racial achievement gap between African American children and white children became a concern in many public school systems. The Oakland Schools set up a task force to study this problem and to recommend solutions to close the racial achievement gap. The task force recommended a new program that was built around language. The Oakland Unified School District in California passed a resolution recognizing Ebonics, a term that is a blend of ebony and phonetics (December 1996). Linguists referred to it as African-American Vernacular English, more commonly known as AAVE.[8]

At the heart of this program, Ebonics was recognized as a legitimate language that honored the language children spoke in their homes. Through Ebonics, Black students could freely express themselves in school using the language and syntax from their homes without being told they were speaking incorrectly. "My sister walk

---

[7] Walt Wolfram, "American Tongues," CNAM, 1987.
[8] "African-American Vernacular English," *Wikipedia*.

yesterday" is not Standard English, although we understand the sentence perfectly.

Ebonics has its own syntax and language rules. The basic principle behind Ebonics is that it is easier to learn another language if you can compare it to the language you already speak. The goal was for African American children to learn Standard English while honoring their own language. Teachers taught students to understand their own language's syntax and how it differed from Standard English.

Ebonics was immediately misunderstood by educators and laypeople alike. A frantic national dialogue ensued. Adding to the firestorm, poet Maya Angelou and the Rev. Jesse Jackson spoke out against the Oakland Schools proposal, thinking that teaching Ebonics to Black students would hold them back from making strides in jobs, education, and other opportunities.[9] Well-meaning educators said Black applicants would be instantly disqualified from interviews due to their nontraditional speech. Others thought of Ebonics as a dual-language approach, where white suburban children would learn to speak Ebonics and Black children would learn to speak *white*.

This was never the intent. Some states passed laws that banned using Ebonics as a teaching tool in the classroom. Critics argued that using Ebonics would disable African American students. How would African Americans interview for a job or apply to college when they spoke Ebonics? Critics didn't understand that through Ebonics, students would learn to speak Standard English by understanding their own language more fully.

Later, Jackson, armed with more information, changed his opinion, saying, "They're not trying to teach Black English as a standard language. They're looking for tools to teach children standard English so they might be competitive."[10]

Eventually, under great pressure, the Oakland School Board abandoned Ebonics, and it disappeared from the curriculum and from national conversations. Ebonics was completely misunderstood

---

[9] "'Black English' Proposal Draws Fire," *CNN*, December 22, 1996, http://www.cnn.com/US/9612/22/black.english/index.html.

[10] Martha Irvine, "Jesse Jackson Takes Back Criticism of Oakland School 'Black English' Plan," *AP News*, December 26, 1996.

and too threatening. Ironically, most educators now understand that a foundational teaching strategy is to build scaffolds to take children from where they are in their learning to where we want them to be.

Language sets expectations about who we are and where we belong. Too often, students who speak the language of their homes are viewed as less intelligent than children who speak Standard English. Schools rank and sort students into levels and learning groups that result in a disproportionate number of Black students being placed in lower groups.

Supporters of Ebonics stated that students who communicate effectively in their own cultural language should be viewed as smart and not belittled because they deviate from the dominant language. Ebonics would have been a powerful teaching tool for many Black students. The threat of a separate language, honored by the school system, made for uncomfortable feelings in the traditional school world. Sandra Garcia said in her presentation "Why We Need Ebonics Now,"

> What the last 20 years have demonstrated, is the sheer scale of the missed opportunity. America's out-of-hand dismissal of AAVE has widened the racial achievement gap, entrenched discrimination and made us all a little more scared of each other. Which raises the simple question: What's keeping us from making another push for AAVE now?[11]

The abandonment of Ebonics stands out as an example of how our attitudes about language and culture flow through and define people. Our language is the first descriptor of who we are and how others see us.

---

[11] Sandra Garcia, "Why We Need Ebonics Now," Vimeo, http://vimeo. com/233578702.

Bluebonics

In my blue-collar home, we used a different language model, one that also deviated from Standard English. My language was learned from my nonschooled parents. In our home, we said, "I seen that," or "He could have went there yesterday." Although there was no racial presence in my small Minnesota elementary school, the result was that I belonged to a stigmatized group. Those of us who spoke "blue-collar language," which I have dubbed *bluebonics*, were thought to be less intelligent than our classmates who came to school with proper subject-verb agreement, supported by educated parents.

My teachers did not understand that my language was sophisticated. It communicated meaning just as well as that of my more privileged classmates—it just was not Standard English. Teachers subconsciously formed impressions about the potential of us "bluebonic kids." My teacher told me that I should be a hairdresser like my mom because I had such pretty curly hair. She told Bruce, whose father was a lawyer, that he should be a college professor or a judge because he was so smart.

When I was twelve, my girlfriend (who had professional parents) said to me, "Why do you talk so funny?" I was startled. For the first time, I recognized that my home language differed from the book learning in my school. My teachers had never pointed out that I spoke differently, probably because they thought that I would forever be relegated to the working-class world and had no need of an excellent grammar background. When children speak differently from the dominant language, they are presumed to be less intelligent. We see people through their language.

Febonics

Blue-collar children and Black children learn the language of their homes, and their language forms perceptions and expectations of both groups, which brings us to Febonics, my metaphor for language about women. The language about women has translated into unconscious bias, even to those who claim to be bias-free. Adrienne Rich said,

> Sexist grammar burns into the brains of little girls and young women a message that the male is the norm, the standard, the central figure beside which we are all deviants, the marginal, the dependent variables.[12]

Words, whether we speak them or hear them, establish the relative value of being a woman. Early feminists believed sexism could be reduced by identifying words that were negatively associated with women. They maintained that language could be reformed by changing the way women were represented in ads, TV, newspapers, and books. This idea was based on the belief that people did not want to be misogynistic, and they would change their sexist vocabulary if it were brought to their attention.

Feminists hold a variety of opinions on this subject. Miranda Fricker argues that marginalized people suffer from *hermeneutical injustice* when they are not able to create the concepts and terms through language to help them understand their own experience. She believes that people in power create linguistic representations of the things that matter to them, not that matter to marginalized groups.[13]

Women, in this case, are the marginalized group. Men regularly use words that are demeaning to women like calling other men *douches* or *douchebags*. Do they know that the purpose of a douche is for cleansing the vagina? Yet rarely is this type of language challenged. A man rebukes another man by labeling him a *son of a bitch* or a *bastard*. These names reflect on a woman's sex life, not a man's. A bastard is technically the child of an unmarried woman, and a son of

---

[12] Adrienne Rich, *On Lies, Secrets and Silence: Selected Prose 1966–1978* (W. W. Norton and Company, 1995), 134.

[13] Miranda Fricker, "Powerlessness and Social Interpretation," *Episteme: A Journal of Social Epistemology* 3, no. 1–2 (2006): pp. 97-99, https://www.sheffield. ac.uk/polopoly_fs/1.152343!/file/3.1fricker.pdf.

a bitch is the male child of a woman who is unpleasant. Few people think about how these words are directly unjust to women.

Sexist language can be overt or passive. Speakers may hold sexist views but never express their views in sexist terms. Sexism can be benevolent, where a man believes he needs to protect a woman out of love because she is weak, less competent, and not able to take care of herself. Or sexism can be hostile, where power and negative feelings fuel the need for a man to keep a woman in her place. Women can be loved, denigrated, and treated hostilely, all under the umbrella of sexism. Sara Mills says,

> In giving voice to sexist language, people align themselves with conservative models of social formation…and a view of women's natural role which is at odds with women's actual roles in contemporary society.[14]

On the other hand, the *absence* of language about women is instructive. Early feminists argued that when masculine nouns and pronouns were used in documents and speech—i.e., *all men are created equal*—they kept women invisible and ignored their position in society. Pronouns like *he* and *man* were used until very recently to refer to people and groups that may or may not include women. *Mankind, freshman*, the *common man*, and *mailman* are examples of groups that include women but where women are rendered invisible by language.

Recently, efforts have been made to become more inclusive by using gender fair language, although some of it is awkward. *Person* often replaces *man*, and *legislator* is used in place of *congressman*. *Star Trek* made the change from "where no man has gone before" to "where no one has gone before." Some changes are slower. My granddaughter is still referred to as a freshman in high school. One signs a master contract and then becomes a master teacher. In Lake Forest,

---

[14] S. Mills, *Language and Sexism* (Cambridge: Cambridge University Press, 2008), 32.

Illinois, the aldermen are the executive officers of the city, even when they are female.

Men's sports provide ample examples of how our vocabulary has been developed by men and around their interests. Benign, nonjudgmental sports phrases have become essential for us to describe our lives and leadership. Terms like *out of bounds, home run, slam dunk, knockout punch, go to the mat*, and *level the playing field* are used by men and women to instruct and explain, with little realization that women are invisible in these examples. There is no robust, equivalent language developed around women and their interests used by both men and women.

One prevailing sexist language strategy is to insult a man by comparing him to a woman. The drill sergeant says to male recruits, "Okay, ladies, form up and run a mile." The baseball coach motivates a boy by saying, "You throw like a girl." The football coach tells kids not to get frustrated, saying, "Don't get your panties in a bunch." When a man is labeled *effeminate*, it suggests that he has characteristics typical of a woman, which is repugnant to most men. No man wants to cry like a girl or be a pussy. The overriding message is that nobody should want to be like a girl. The language of weakness is about women. The language of strength is about men. The culture of language reinforces societal norms that view women as weak, subservient, and sexually servile.

In 1968, Virginia Slims launched an ad campaign aimed at attracting women smokers. Their motto was, "You've Come a Long Way, Baby." They presented a list of clichés that they wanted to drop into the English language, including "One small step for woman, one giant step for womankind," "We hold these truths to be self-evident: that all women are created equal," and "A woman's home is her castle." The advertising campaign concluded with "After all, when you have your own slim cigarette, you really deserve your own clichés, too."[15] The message was about language. But these clichés did

---

[15] "Virginia Slims Cigarettes, 1971," Vintage Ads, http://oldadvertising.blogspot. com/2009/09/virginia-slims-cigarettes-1971.html.

not drop into our language, even with a well-funded ad campaign, nor did other clichés get reformed that bent women's way.

Fifty years after the Virginia Slims ad, in 2020, an Allstate Insurance TV commercial shows the "mayhem man," saying to a woman, "Do you always drive like a little old lady?"

She insults him back by saying, "*You* drive like a little old lady."

Confusingly, this ad uses a woman to insult a man by insulting women.

A common practice is the difference in how men and women are asked for information when they sign in for accounts or tickets. Females may choose the titles of Mrs., Miss, or Ms., presumably to reveal their marital status. A male, on the other hand, only selects Mr., which sheds no light onto whether he is married. Other choices for name selection are now more common to all, such as *unidentified*, or *wish not to disclose*.

Mrs Man is the title of a study by Una Stannard (1977) that traced the centuries-old practice of calling married women by their husband's first and surname names—i.e., Mrs. Joe Doe, which leaves no trace of the wife and only represents her husband.[16] These invisible women's identities flow from their husbands. Even words defining marriage as "man and wife" imply ownership. Parallel construction is "husband and wife" or "man and woman."

Vocabulary and its enduring impact on the perception of women was the subject of a book entitled *Sexism and Language* (1977). An example given by the authors was words that labelled women as things. "Because of our expectations of passivity, we like to compare females to items that people acquire for pleasure." The authors talk about women being compared to food like a dish, a cookie, a tart, or a sweetie pie. They also noted that girls were often compared to plants: a clinging vine, a shrinking violet, or a wallflower.[17] Men are rarely compared to pastries or plants.

---

[16] Una Stannard, *Mrs Man* (San Francisco, CA: Germainbooks, 1977), 195–200.

[17] Alleen Nilsen, Haig Bosmajan, H. Lee Gershuny, and Julia Stanley, *Sexism and Language* (National Council of Teachers of English, 1977), 32.

I was inspired to explore today's language to gauge what progress has been made toward a "level playing field." I took the bull by the horns (the cow by the teats?). My small research project started by asking ten men to name slang words they use for vagina. Most were uncomfortable with the question and reluctantly said *cunt* or *pussy*, with a few saying, "The C-word" or "The P-word."

One man added, "I won't say them in present company." I was the present company.

Another man said, "I can't really think of any."

When I asked the same men to list slang for penis and testicles, they had much more to draw upon: balls, nuts, junk, dick, cock, pecker, package, johnson, rocks, and family jewels. These names did not spark embarrassment, need to be represented by a letter, or not be said in present company.

I asked ten women the same questions. They came up with the same slang for penis and testicles. When it came to vagina, however, women used markedly different language from men. None said *cunt*, *pussy*, or *twat*. They said *vajayay*, *lady parts*, *girly parts*—with little agreed-upon terminology. I tried to imagine a man talking to his bar buddies saying, "My wife needs a test on her girly parts."

My small sample suggests women are not equipped with language that helps navigate the awkward waters of female genitalia. We live in a society where norms define us, and they are perpetuated by language. Noah Webster said in 1817, "A living language must keep pace with improvements in knowledge and with the multiplication of ideas."[18] Women have not kept pace with the multiplication of ideas about themselves.

Thinking of other examples of nonequivalent language was easy. A cranky woman is said to be "on the rag." This word has expanded to a verb: "she is ragging on me." *Bitch* is an especially flexible word, one said frequently about women and used by both men and women. In noun form, a woman can be "a bitch on wheels," or she can have a

---

[18] Noah Webster, "A Letter to the Honorable John Pickering, on the Subject of His Vocabulary; or Collection of Words and Phrases, Supposed to Be Peculiar to the United States of American" (Boston: West and Richardson, 1817).

"bitch fest" or an "rbf" (resting bitch face). As an adjective, a woman can be bitchy. The word *bitch* is so versatile, it can also be used to compliment: ("Hey, bitch, you did great") or denigrate ("You're my bitch," which is usually said by a man who has bested another man).

Unequivocal language is built into our norms. When we talk about growing a pair, we are not referring to breasts. When a woman dominates a man, he is pussy-whipped. Conversely, when a man dominates a woman, she is not dick-whipped. Who has heard of a wife "rooster-pecking" her husband? A woman can be a ball buster, but a man is never a vajajay buster. A woman who wears the pants in the family is considered aggressive and overbearing. Men never wear the dress in the family, even when they are helpful with children, cooking, and chores. There is no phrase that captures the idea of a man dominating his wife because the cultural expectation has long held that it is his rightful position.

The lack of equivalency between men and women's language is endless. Women have penis envy, but men do not have vagina envy (as in the Freudian sense). No old bachelors in the popcorn. Animal names are disproportionally used to denigrate women. Women are catty, nags, and batty. An overweight woman is a heifer. A girl who is not pretty is a dog or has a horse face. A woman is a shrew, while a man is shrewd. Words that describe women's personalities are hormonal, gossipy, battle-ax, ditzy, pushy, abrasive, shrill, clingy, aggressive, old bag, hysterical, and bossy.

Why do women use the same demeaning language as men do about women? Perhaps it is an effort to desensitize sexist language so that it loses its ability to form underlying judgments. Or women may want to show they belong to the boys' club. Or women don't make the connection that these words are sexist. Are women inconsistent when they use language that defines them as second-class citizens and then complain they are treated like second-class citizens?

Most feminists agree that concepts like male as the norm, invisibility of women, false gender neutrality, and the maleness of our language contribute to a lack of resources for women to express and understand their own experience in our society. Sexist language reflects the heart of the problem. People's attitudes are revealed in the language they use. Often, people who use sexist language are not aware of their underlying bias.

Febonics is about raising awareness of our language and the metaphors about women and, in some cases, men. Men named Dick have suffered unnecessarily from a society willing to take a person's name and cruelly align it with genitals and use it to describe annoying men. *Brandon* is linked to liberal politics and used sarcastically by the those who embrace politics from the right. *Karen* has become synonymous with demanding and difficult. We need to refrain from using hurtful language that demeans others.

The following was sent to me by a guy out there who thinks this is funny:

Hahaha.
This is for all ladies to enjoy.
Women has Man in it.
Mrs. has Mr. in it.
Female has Male in it.
She has He in it.
Madam has Adam in it.
Ever noticed how all women's
problems start with men?
MENtal illness.
MENstrual cramps.
MENtal breakdown. MENopause.
GUYnecologist. & when we have
REAL trouble, it's a HISterectolmy!
Send this 2 all women U know to
Brighten their thoughts.
Cheers to our patience.

That certainly brightened my thoughts! I wrote *Woman Up!*, thinking it would have broad appeal, but I hope men will enjoy it too.

Euripides, the Greek poet and playwright who lived in 400 BC, said, "This is slavery, not to speak one's thought." Women are challenged to be informed and speak their thoughts. All have an ethical obligation to woman up when the dignity of others is denied.

Take the Febonic challenge: count the number of times in two days you can identify words that are unflattering to women. Don't get hysterical. Don't be a sissy. Go to the mat. Woman up! Take the challenge.

CHAPTER 2

Professional Women

We teach girls that they can have ambition, but not too much,
to be successful, but not too successful, or they'll threaten men.
—Chimamanda Ngozi Adichie,
We Should All Be Feminists

A taste of feminism

I gave up being an amateur woman and became a newly minted professional woman when I signed on as a high school art teacher. There, as a new teacher, I encountered my first experience with feminist activism: the pants rebellion, a little-known event that occurred at my high school in 1971. A group of about twenty women teachers staged a protest by wearing—wait for it—slacks and pantsuits to school.

We secretly planned the uprising for weeks, solemnly promising to our sisters-in-legs that on a specific day in January, we would all dress in slacks or pantsuits to protest being forced to be dress-wearers. Proudly, not one of us deviated from the sacred oath, and on the appointed day, we appeared together with metaphorically linked legs. We waited all day for repercussions. There were none. Nobody seemed to care. We asked ourselves several questions. Had we actually been told we could not wear pants? Might we have imposed societal rules and norms where none existed? Did we assume there were obstacles where none existed? We were not sure.

We perceived an inequity, conceived a plan to change rules, organized like-minded people, and acted. We had participated in our first feminist challenge, even though we were uncertain about our original grievance, but we knew we had experienced our first taste of feminism.

While teaching, I became pregnant with my second child, who was born in 1972. One day, early in my pregnancy, I was asked to report to the superintendent's office, where he told me that I needed to quit teaching when I began "to show." He explained that women did not continue teaching much after three months of pregnancy. He added, "What will the high school boys think?"

I did not quit and no one approached me again. I concluded that the superintendent must have rethought his position because I was an exemplary teacher. I continued teaching until I had my baby in April and resumed teaching the following August. The high school boys did just fine. With certainty, I knew the administration fully backed me because I was an outstanding teacher.

In an unusual turn of events, I became superintendent of this same school district fourteen years after I left as a teacher. As the new superintendent, I could not resist pulling my personnel file from my former teaching years and checking what was in it. There, I found an attorney's letter. Unknown to me, the school district had consulted an attorney when I was pregnant with my second child in 1972. The school district asked the attorney if I could be forced to leave. The attorney informed the administration that a new law called Title IX was about to be passed.

Title IX was signed into law by Richard Nixon on July 23, 1972, three months after the birth of my daughter. Although most people think of this law as one having mostly to do with sports, it states that "no person in the United States shall, of the basis of sex…be denied the benefits of, or be subjected to discrimination under any education program or activity receiving Federal financial assistance." The attorney recommended that I be allowed to continue teaching because of the likely consequences of this new law.

When my third child was born in 1977, there was no reference to forcing pregnant women to quit. This birth also coincided with important legislation. The Pregnancy Discrimination Act of 1978 amended Title VII of the Civil Rights Act of 1964, stating that "women affected by pregnancy, childbirth or related medical conditions, shall be treated the same for all employment-related purposes, including receipt of fringe benefits."

After reading my personnel file, I realized that my assumption about being allowed to continue teaching because I was a terrific teacher was wrong. Actually, a group of dedicated feminists had been fighting for laws that protected me both in 1972 and in 1978. I had credited my talent, when in truth, I was ignorant of and ungrateful to the women and men who waged tireless battles to protect my rights and equality.

When women lead

After teaching for ten years, I decided to apply for a leadership position. I knew no women mentors, but I had heard about the *Women's Dress for Success* book by John T. Molloy (1977). Molloy advised aspiring women to dress for the job they wanted, not the one they had. The book stated that interviewees should dress like the person who would interview them and like the person who would be their boss, predictably, a man.

Consequently, when I interviewed for my first leadership job, I wore a black suit with padded shoulders, a matching pencil skirt, a white no-frill blouse, and a silk scarf tied into a bow around my neck ostensibly to imitate a man's tie. Also, I carried a briefcase, which I thought added a nice touch, although it was empty. It was a balancing act to woman/man dress, but I did it, and the advice was good for that time. As an aside, Dress for Success has become a nationwide organization that supports women who may not have available resources for professional wardrobe. Women donate professional clothes they no longer need for the benefit of other women. That's *real* dress for success.[19]

The next time I interviewed for an administrative position, I had plenty of leadership experience under my silk bow. I wore my own choice of clothes—soft colors and feminine lines. Feedback from the interview committee suggested they worried that I wasn't savvy. After all, what woman would dress like a woman for a job interview?

By then, I was comfortable not pretending to lead like a man. As I recall, the issue of my choice of clothing was of higher priority with the interview committee than my leadership style or curriculum expertise. Women who work in a man's world have often tried to emulate men's thinking and behavior. They reason that men are successful because, ipso facto, they are men.

Once, a male supervisor told me, in what assuredly was a compliment, "You think more like a man than a woman." Some women have enjoyed their special membership in the "boys' club" and want to reserve their status as the single woman who was accepted into the fellowship. Women in executive positions often remain shackled by the notion that good leaders should act like men. Breaking from the mold of trying to win the title of honorary man and embracing the unique qualities that women bring to leadership was a transitional time for me.

Women's leadership: what we know

In their 2020 article "7 Leadership Lessons Men Can Learn from Women," *Harvard Business Review* authors Tomas Chamorro-Premuzik and Cindy Gallop suggest that many people believe women's underrepresentation in leadership would be solved if women would lead the same way that men lead. Yet the authors say that men's leadership record is not overly impressive. They posit that the average woman has more potential for leadership than the average man. Women tend to show more empathy and humility than men,

---

[19] DressForSuccess.org.

and they are more interested in establishing emotional connections and coaching. Their conclusion is that we should ask men to adopt some of the more effective skills of women rather than the other way around.[20]

In 2011, Dr. Jack Zenger and Dr. Joseph Folkman set out to research the ways that leadership styles vary between men and women. Their survey included the responses of 7,280 leaders from successful and progressive organizations that included those from public, private, government, commercial, domestic, and international sectors. Zenger and Folkman created sixteen competencies related to overall leadership effectiveness for their rankings. Some findings were surprising and some, not so much.

In the not-so-surprising category, the majority of the top leaders of their organizations were men (78 percent). Women were better represented as jobs became less prestigious and lower on the organizational chart. In the very surprising category, women outscored men in fifteen of sixteen leadership competencies in the survey. The largest gap was in the category Takes Initiative, with women outscoring men by almost 12 percent. Practices Self-Development was the next largest gap where women outscored men by 11 percent.

The one area where men ranked higher than women was Develops Strategic Perspective but only by three percentage points. With the results in hand, Zenger and Folkman said,

> As leaders in organizations look hard to find the talent they need to achieve exceptional results, they ought to be aware that many women have impressive leadership skills.

---

[20] Tomas Chamorro-Premuzik and Cindy Gallop, "7 Leadership Lessons Men Can Learn from Women," *Harvard Business Review*, April 1, 2020, https://hbr.org/2020/04/7-leadership-lessons-men-can-learn-from-women.

They also added, "Clearly, chauvinism or discrimination is an enigma that organizations (and the business culture) should work hard to prevent."[21]

Women Political Leaders (WPL), a global network of women politicians, teamed with Kantar, a worldwide data, insights, and consulting company, to develop The Reykjavik Index for Leadership supported by the Bill & Melinda Gates Foundation. The index measures how comfortable societies are with women's leadership in the G7 countries: Canada, France, Germany, Italy, Japan, United States, and the UK. The study was replicated in India, Kenya, and Nigeria. It included more than twenty-two thousand working-age people across twenty-two industries and public professions.

Canada and France were listed as the countries with the most equal perception of men and women leaders in 2020–21. The United States was third on the index in general comfort with women's leadership, behind Canada and the UK. The United States gained one point on the index, from seventy-five in 2019 to seventy-six in 2020, indicating the level of comfort level with women's leadership is rising very slightly.

Women, in every country studied, were more likely than men to view both genders equally suitable for leadership. Accordingly, US women support having a woman as the head of their government (70 percent) more than men (54 percent). Key findings of the report showed that almost one in ten US boards have no women members. Another finding was that during the pandemic, women lost more jobs than men across all sectors. Although women make up 46 percent of the workforce, they accounted for 55 percent of the jobs lost in March and April 2020.[22]

---

[21] Jack Zenger and Joseph Folkman, "Are Women Better Leaders than Men," *Harvard Business Review*, March 15, 2017, https://hbr.org/2012/03/a-study-in-leadership-women-do.

[22] "The Reykjavik Index for Leadership," WPL and Kantar, 2020-2021, https://www.kantar.com/campaigns/reykjavik-index.

Silvana Koch-Mehrin, president and founder of Women Political Leaders said,

> The launch of the [Reykjavik] Index in 2018 enabled conversations, not just on the where and how women aren't viewed equally, but on the why. With the continuation of the evidence provided by the Reykjavik Index and a global community of purpose, both public policy and the private sector can further progress to equity in leadership.[23]

Noted early in the COVID-19 battle was the response of women presidents to manage and make decisions that benefitted their countries. Avivah Wittenberg-Cox contrasted the leadership of women leaders to the male leadership of strongmen, who used the pandemic crisis to increase their authoritarianism by blaming and shaming others:

> There have been years of research timidly suggesting that women's leadership styles might be different and beneficial. Instead, too many political organizations and companies are still working to get women to behave more like men if they want to lead or succeed. Yes, these national leaders are case study sightings of the seven leadership traits men may want to learn from women. It's time we recognized it—and elected more of it.[24]

---

[23] Ibid.

[24] Avivah Wittenberg-Cox, "What Do Countries with the Best Coronavirus Responses Have in Common? Women Leaders," *Forbes*, April 13, 2020, https://www.forbes.com/sites/avivahwittenbergcox/2020/04/13/what-do-countries-with-the-best-coronavirus-reponses-have-in-common-women-leaders/?sh=db227a93dec4.

Embedded in the research about men and women's leadership is the underlying question of what we value. Soraya Chemaly tweeted on April 17, 2020,

> The point about women leaders isn't that they are magical beings or feminine superheroes. The point is that their leadership is a resounding commentary on the values of the societies that elect them.[25]

As we look at questions of leadership, perhaps women embrace the values of their larger society more frequently than men.

A personal path

My career path included employment as an elementary principal, high school principal, and school superintendent. Women high school principals were uncommon in large Chicago suburban high schools in 1984. The day my appointment was announced as the new high school principal, concerns were immediate. How could a woman handle sports? How could a woman take on male employees who needed to be disciplined? How could she deal with high school boys who were bigger than she was? My superintendent understood that leadership is about people, programs, and policies and that good decisions are made by people who can reason, collaborate, and are grounded in their beliefs.

While at the high school, I hired a female security monitor, whose job was to know the kids and ask them to mind the rules in the cafeteria, at the basketball games, etc. She reviewed the job description and accepted the position. All went fine until the first basketball game, where she was expected to hold a retaining rope as people entered and exited the basketball court area to isolate the basketball players from the crowd. She did not want to do that part

---

[25] Sorara Chemaly (@schemaly), Twitter, April 17, 2020.

of the job, so she told me she couldn't do it because her husband wouldn't let her.

Around the same time, a friend of mine told me she had been asked to fundraise for a charity where she served as a board member. She confided that she was not comfortable asking people for money, so she told the executive director that her husband wouldn't let her fundraise.

Later, when I had been appointed as the new superintendent of my former school district, I experienced a sharp reminder about the difference between a woman's perspective and that of my male colleagues. One evening, our school was hosting a girls' gymnastics competition. I was working in my office when I heard a knock on the door. A desperate girl gymnast from the visiting team was visibly happy when a woman opened the door. "Please," she said, "I have an emergency. I just got my period, and I have to perform in twenty minutes. There are no tampon machines in your school's bathrooms."

I was astounded. I had never thought to check the girls' bathrooms for tampon machines. What high school, where 50 percent of the students menstruate, wouldn't have tampon machines? I had several tampons in my purse and gave them to the grateful gymnast.

The next day, I approached the administrator in charge of facilities and asked him why there were no tampon machines in the girls' bathrooms. "Girls should be prepared," he replied. "There's no reason why they can't plan ahead."

I replied, "In a perfect world, that might be true, but these are high school girls, and they can't always rely on their bodies to be completely predictable. Please order tampon machines immediately and have them installed in every girls' bathrooms."

I could see the irritated thought-balloon floating over his head: *This is what happens when a woman is in charge.*

Representation of women

Women continue to spread their wings. More women are in the United States Air Force (USAF) than in any other military branch, although when a woman enlists in the air force, she becomes an airman. Females currently make up 21 percent of the air force membership but represent only 7.5 percent of officers at the level of brigadier general or higher. When RAND Corporation asked female nonrated officers why they left the air force at greater numbers than their male counterparts, they cited several reasons. Issues related to children were frequently noted: maternity leave, breastfeeding accommodations, adequate childcare on military bases, and rigid timelines with little flexibility.

Women also talked about sexism and the "old boys' network."[26] In response, the air force has undertaken a number of woman-friendly initiatives to address their needs.[27] Maternity leave is now twelve weeks, and women are given a year after birth before deployment and fitness tests. The Career Intermission Program allows for partial pay for up to three years before a woman comes back to active duty after giving birth. Height and weight charts have been standardized and now apply equally to men and women. Even the air force song, which begins, "Off we go into the wild blue yonder," has been modified. The third verse, which was also the academy's school song, previously began, "Here's a toast to the host…To a friend we send a message of his brother men who fly." Air Force Chief of Staff General Dave Goldfein felt a change was needed to include female members. Now the third verse is, "To a friend we send a message of the brave who serve on high."[28]

Good steps forward, then two steps back. Tucker Carlson, Fox News host, March 11, 2021, said that Biden is making a mockery of the military by making it more feminine. He was referring to new designs for maternity wear for women who are pregnant. Military

---

[26] Miriam Mathews, "The Air Force Is Working Hard to Retain Female Officers, and Here's How," *The RAND Blog*, August 6, 2018, https://www.rand.org/blog/2018/08/the-us-air-force-is-working-harder-to-retain-female.html.

[27] Ibid.

[28] Oriana Pawlyk, "The Air Force Has Updated Its Song to Be Gender-Neutral," *Military.com*, February 27, 2020, https://www.military.com/daily-news/2020/02/27/air-force-has-updated-its-song-be-gender-neutral.html.

leaders were fast to call Carlson out for insulting a man by calling him feminine.[29]

When women and men are equally represented in the rank and file, they are generally underrepresented as leaders. Seventy-two percent of K–12 educators are women, yet about 85 percent of our nation's almost fourteen thousand school superintendents were men in 2016. A host of reasons is given for this small number: women do not want the job, they do not have suitable credentials, and they may enter the profession too late. Thomas Glass, on the other hand, says the two widely cited reasons for the low number of women school superintendents is that women are discouraged from preparing for the superintendent's position, and school boards won't hire them.[30]

Like the air force, various organizations have developed new policies to improve equal opportunities for women. Symphony orchestras have instituted "blind auditions," where performers audition behind a screen. A committee chooses the successful person without knowing the gender of the person who wins the audition. But in a list of the top 150 symphony conductors in the world, only five were women in 2018.[31] Even more flagrant, women composed 1.3 percent of works performed by professional orchestras in the United States in the 2016–17 season, according to data from the Baltimore Symphony Orchestra.[32]

The uphill climb over time for women in music was illustrated by a recital by Käbi Laretei, world-renowned pianist, given at the

---

[29] Ryan Pickrell, "Pentagon Tells Tucker Carlson It Won't Take Advice from a Talk-Show Host after He Complained Biden Is Making Military 'More Feminine'" Yahoo! News, March 11, 2021, https://news.yahoo.com/pentagon-tells-tucker-carlson-wont-171918188.html.

[30] Thomas Glass, "The Study of the American School Superintendency," AAA, 2000, https://eric.ed.gov/?id=ED440475.

[31] Hazel Rowland, "Why Are There So Few Female Conductors?" *Culture Trip*, December 7, 2016, https://theculturetrip.com/europe/united-kingdom/articles/where-are-all-the-women-conductors/.

[32] Darcel Rockett, "'It's All from the Same Dead White Guys': Meet the Chicagoans Pushing for Gender Equity in Classical Music," *Chicago Tribune*, Mary 22, 2019, https://www.chicagotribune.com/lifestyles/ct-life-chicago-sinfonietta-project-w-20190322-story.html.

Eastman School of Music on March 14, 1967. *The New York Times* review said that she played brilliantly and was one of the prettiest pianists appearing on stage. Laretei was married to Ingmar Bergman, the great Swedish filmmaker. The difference in how these great artists were represented is a reminder of how beauty was considered an essential part of a woman's value.

Women are still the primary cooks in family homes. According to the America Time Use Survey from 2003 to 2016, college-educated women cooked 69 percent of the time in their homes in 2016, while women with less than a high school education cooked 72 percent of the time.[33] Logic follows that women should be more highly represented as chefs, yet less than 7 percent of restaurants in the US are led by female chefs.[34]

Choose a profession. Women are generally underrepresented in all top positions regardless of the gender representation in the field. Are women less musical? Do they have fewer culinary skills? Are they not able to understand leadership? Or have stereotypes in these fields continued to be reinforced and perpetuated on the basis of sex?

Men and women see discrimination facing women differently, depending on the business area. In a 2018 online survey of 1,010 people in the entertainment field, a deep unconscious bias was present. Twenty-six percent of women working in Hollywood agreed with the statement "At my company, men and women working at the same level are paid the same," while a majority of men (56 percent) agreed with the statement. Another sharp difference in perception was 36 percent of women, and 57 percent of men agreed with the statement that they are promoted at equal rates. Surprisingly, when the results of this survey were compared to a similar survey of financial service workers, the people on Wall Street saw less gender bias than those in Hollywood.[35]

---

[33] L. S. Taillie, "Who's Cooking? Trends in US Home Food Preparation by Gender, Education, and Race/Ethnicity from 2003 to 2016," *Nutrition Journal* 17, no. 41 (2018), https://www.ncbi.nlm.nih.gov/pmc/articles/PMC5881182/.

[34] Ibid.

[35] Julia Boorstin, "After Time's Up and #MeToo, Women in Entertainment Still See Gender Issues that Men Don't," CNBC, October 29, 2018, https://www.

State Senator Hannah-Beth Jackson said that one-fourth of California's publicly traded companies do not have a female on their boards despite independent studies that show companies are more profitable and productive with woman board members.[36] California passed a law that mandates the state can no longer have publicly traded firms with all-male boards, and by 2021, boards with six or more directors will need to have two women.

Childcare

Finding quality, affordable childcare remains a challenging experience for women who work outside the home, and basically, they are on their own. Throughout our history, women have had to find childcare by asking parents, friends, older siblings, or using creative methods to figure it out.

In 2020, COVID-19 complicated the issue even more. Childcare emerged as the top concern for people in the pandemic. Battles ensued with many parents demanding that schools reopen, in part, because working parents have looked to them to fill the role of taking care of children. Our solutions for affordable, quality childcare have improved little over time. Patricia Cole, director of government relations within Zero to Three, a nonprofit focused on early childhood development, said, "Childcare is foundational to our nation's ability to recover from this crisis [pandemic]."[37]

Childcare has a mixed history from the earliest times in the United States. The first efforts focused on poor mothers in the early part of the twentieth century. Charity was viewed as the appropriate

---

cnbc.com/2018/10/26/after-metoo-women-in-entertainment-still-see-issues-that-men-dont.html.

[36] Vanessa Fuhrman and Alejandro Lazo, "California Moves to Mandate Female Board Directors," *The Wall Street Journal*, August 29, 2018, https://www.wsj.com/articles/california-moves-to-mandate-female-board-directors-1535571904.

[37] Jessica Guynn, "Coronavirus Child Care Crisis Tops Concerns as Nation Pushes to Reopen. Parents Ask: Who Will Watch Our Children?" *USA Today*, May 17, 2020, https://www.usatoday.com/story/money/2020/05/17/coronavirus-childcare-america-reopening-trump-fauci/5194811002/.

way to support poor and fatherless families. But charity giving was sporadic and unreliable. In some cases, mothers coped by giving their children to orphanages. By 1912, Jane Addams and her supporters advocated for widows' pensions and mothers' pensions. These pensions were benefits paid from the state that *required* women to stay at home with their families. Addams believed that poor women were being forced to work in low-paying jobs and forced to leave their children in inadequate childcare situations.

Opponents of the mothers' and widows' pensions believed that public tax money should *not* be spent to support women, who were often poor and sometimes considered immoral. A small group had a differing opinion altogether. They felt that women were deprived of making their own choices.

Unfortunately, women needed to decide between working or staying at home. They could not receive a pension unless they stayed home. By 1930, almost every state had widows' or mothers' pensions, with promoters and dissenters on both sides of the issue. Harry Hopkins, who would later become the eighth secretary of commerce and President Theodore Roosevelt's closest advisor, depicted the dilemma in 1914: "There is always the danger that in our dread of making people dependent, we shall cease to do good for fear of doing harm."[38]

Childcare became a focus for the federal government for the first time in World War II. The government made a huge recruitment effort for women to work in jobs vacated by men joining the war effort. Employing women addressed the job crisis, but it resulted in a childcare crisis. Between 1940 and 1945, 350,000 women served in the armed forces, and five million women joined the workforce.

By 1943, more women than men worked in the aircraft industry. Adequate childcare became an emergency. At the urging of Eleanor Roosevelt, Congress interpreted the Lanham Act (1943), which had been passed two years earlier, to include support for childcare in "war impacted areas." An estimated two million places were needed for

---

[38] June Hopkins, *Harry Hopkins: Sudden Hero, Brash Reformer* (New York, NY: St. Martin's Press, 1991), 91.

childcare during this period. However, only three thousand centers were opened throughout the country, which served 130,000 children. After V-J Day, most of the childcare centers were shuttered within two years as women left jobs that were given back to men.[39]

Not all segments of American society agreed with women taking jobs in the war effort. According to Doris Kearns Goodwin, *The Catholic World Report* published an editorial in 1943 that stated,

> Women who maintain jobs outside their homes…weaken family life, endanger their own marital happiness, rob themselves of man's protective capabilities, and by consequence, decrease the number of children.[40]

Finding quality childcare has remained an issue. The pandemic moved childcare concerns to a crisis level in the US. Still, solutions are not being developed, and experience tells us that after the pandemic, we will return to business as usual: tapping relatives, finding friends, and using schools to address the need.

A Better Balance, an advocacy group for families and caregivers, reported in 2019 on the effectiveness of federal lawsuits where women have lost two-thirds of their accommodation cases due to pregnancy. Forty percent of women are the family breadwinner, and when they are pushed out of jobs by pregnancy, they often spiral into poverty. Additionally, women take an average 4 percent pay reduction in pay per child. One quarter of women go back to work within two weeks of giving birth because they are not guaranteed paid time off to recover from childbirth.[41]

---

[39] Sonya Michel, "The History of Child Care in the US," *Social Welfare History Project*, 2011, https://socialwelfare.library.vcu.edu/programs/child-care-the-american-history/

[40] Doris Kearns Goodwin, *No Ordinary Time: Franklin & Eleanor Roosevelt: The Home Front in World War II* (Simon and Schuster, 1994), 414.

[41] Michelle Budig, "The Fatherhood Bonus and the Motherhood Penalty: Parenthood and the Gender Gap in Pay," ThirdWay.org, September 2, 2014,

Although men would like to take more time off for parental leave, they often don't because their companies will not pay for leave. Women need recovery time from giving birth, but there is also the automatic assumption that women are the primary childcare givers in the family. Women have a cultural pressure to take parental leave, while men face heavy pressure to take no leave or shorter leaves. Overall, the gender gap shows more mothers (40 percent) taking unpaid leave for caregiving than fathers (24 percent).[42]

As a country, we do not place high value on parental leave for building better families and providing nurturing structures for children. Rather, we place higher value on quickly getting mothers and fathers back to work.

Equal pay

I was born after the war when my father returned from the navy. I grew up with women who had worked throughout the war and then were expected to return to their household duties. I remember my mother and her friend Emma discussing their jobs over coffee one day. Emma, who had worked in a factory job (something to do with plucking chickens, as I recall) said that even though she wanted to keep her job, it just didn't feel right because a man might want to fill it.

My mother did not have the same hard decision. She was a hairdresser, and at that time, men did not compete with women for that job. My mother worked the entire time I was growing up. She encouraged her daughters to work after marriage and to be financially independent. She stressed, "You never know what will happen in life, and you'll be better off if you can make a living." She was a strong feminist and had a great influence on my thinking. We did

---

https://www.thirdway.org/report/the-fatherhood-bonus-and-the-motherhood-penalty-parenthood-and-the-gender-gap-in-pay.

[42] Emily Peck, "Even When Men Take Parental Leave, They're Paid More, New Study Finds," *HuffPost*, December 4, 2019, https://www.huffpost.com/entry/parental-leave-pay-gap_n_5de6ca97e4b00149f73759fc.

have one continuing problem: she wanted to fix my hair in a style that I considered two generations removed.

In my small town, as elsewhere in the country at that time, women were paid less than men for the same job. One of the women in the bakery where I worked explained to me that men deserved more money for the same job because they were the heads of the households. I was surprised she felt that way. She was about fifty years old and was a single head-of-the-household mother, supporting two children. That year (1962), women made fifty-nine cents for every dollar that men earned. Women did not see themselves worthy of equal pay with men even when they shouldered the same burdens.

One hero for equal pay was Billie Jean King, who won six hundred dollars in Rome at the Foro Italico tennis tournament in 1970. Ilie Năstase, the men's winner, took home 3,500 dollars in prize money in the same tournament. King's discontent was evident when she said, "Everyone thinks women should be thrilled when we get crumbs, and I want women to have the cake, the icing and the cherry on top, too."[43]

King famously said she would boycott the 1973 US Tennis Open unless the pay between women and men was equal. That year, the US Open conceded and paid equal prize money to women and men. King founded the Women's Tennis Association (WTA) that year, and she has been a champion in tennis and for equal pay. Finally, in 2006, the Grand Slam made history when the French Open paid equal prize money to women and men.

Still, tennis, as other sports, continues to have gender pay discrepancies in many categories. Ironically, women's tennis has increased TV viewership for men's tennis. From 2010 to 2014, women's tennis was watched more than men's tennis.

Lilly Ledbetter is one of the best-known women who challenged her employer for equal pay. She worked for Goodyear Tire and Rubber for nineteen years. One day, she received an anonymous

---

[43] Atri Bhatt, "WOW! Unleashing the Truth behind Billie Jean King's Breathtaking Achievement at Battle of Sexes," *EssentiallySports*, September 9, 2021, https://www.essentiallysports.com/wta-tennis-news-wow-unleashing-the-truth-behind-billie-jean-kings-breathtaking-achievement-at-battle-of-sexes/

letter, saying she was making thousands of dollars less per year than men working in the same job with the same experience and seniority. In 1997, Ledbetter was working as an area manager, and she was paid an average of 3,727 dollars less per month than her fifteen male counterparts.

Ledbetter sued Goodyear based on violation of Title VII of the Civil Rights Act of 1964, which prohibited pay differences based on gender. She first won and then lost her case on appeal to the Supreme Court (*Ledbetter v. Goodyear Tire & Rubber Co.* 550 US 618 [2007]). The court denied her claim because the action had not been filed within the required 180 days from the date of the discriminatory policy that led to her reduced paycheck.[44]

Supreme Court Justice Ruth Bader Ginsburg wrote the dissent, calling the majority ruling out of tune with the realities of wage discrimination and suggested "that the legislature may act to correct this Court's parsimonious reading of Title VII."[45] The first bill President Obama signed in his presidency was the Lilly Ledbetter Fair Pay Act of 2009. This bill restarted the 180-day clock every time a discriminatory paycheck was issued. Ledbetter never received compensation from Goodyear, but she said, "I'll be happy if the last thing they say about me after I die, is that I made a difference."[46]

On Equal Pay Day, April 2, 2019, women and men were polled about their perceptions of the pay gap. Eighty-three percent of women believed that the pay inequality was true, while 61 percent of men thought the pay gap was "fake news."[47] As usual, perceptions between women and men differ.

---

[44] "Lilly Ledbetter," *Wikipedia.org*.

[45] Ibid.

[46] Sasha Zients, "Lilly Ledbetter: RBG's Dissent in Landmark Case Still Gives Me Chills," CNN, August 22, 2018.

[47] David Harrison and Soo Oh, "Women Work More and Sleep Less: Labor Department's Annual Time Use Survey Highlights the Challenges for Working Women," *The Wall Street Journal*, June 20, 2019, https://www.wsj.com/articles/women-workinglonger-hours-sleeping-less-labor-department-finds-11560980344.

According to the labor department's annual time use survey (2019),

> Women continue to face workplace hardships such as fewer promotions, less support, and implicit bias. They experience pregnancy discrimination, exclusion from the so-called "boys club" and sexual harassment.

Women slept less and worked longer hours on their jobs than they did in 2018. They also spent a half hour more per day than men on household chores and caring for their children.[48] On top of that, they are getting paid eighty cents on average for every dollar a man makes, a trend that's expected to continue through the twenty-third century.[49] During the early days of COVID-19, a humorous tweet aptly summarized the pay gap issue: "This quarantine is affecting everyone in the workforce, but it especially sucks for men. We're losing $1 for every $0.79 women are losing."[50]

The pandemic has affected women disproportionally. Economists have stated that this has been our nation's first female recession. Women of color and women with young children have been particularly hard hit. The gains made by women in recent years have been wiped out by the pandemic through loss of jobs, promotions, and income.[51]

Unfortunately, once there was only a wage gap. Now, women also experience a debt gap. Overall, women heads of household carry

---

[48] David Harrison and Soo Oh, "Women Work More and Sleep Less: Labor Department's Annual Time Use Survey Highlights the Challenges for Working Women," *The Wall Street Journal*, June 20, 2019, https://www.wsj.com/articles/women-workinglonger-hours-sleeping-less-labor-department-finds-11560980344.

[49] Jon Schwartz and Charisse Jones, "The Pay Gap Could Vanish for All Women—Sometime in the 23rd Century," *USA Today*, March 13, 2020.

[50] ilicough (@_RyanKirk), Twitter, March 22, 2020.

[51] Olivia Rockeman, Reade Pickert, and Catarina Saraiva, "The First Female Recession Threatens to Wipe Out Decades of Progress for U.S. Women," Bloomberg, September 30, 2020, https://www.bloombergquint.com/global-economics/u-s-recovery-women-s-job-losses-will-hit-entire-economy.

more debt than men. Women cannot keep up with expenses when their pay is not equal to men's.

Tucker Carlson believes that women who are financially successful are contributing to the decline of men across the country. On a segment of his show on Fox TV, he used unnamed studies to support his claim that women who make more money than men create societal problems for the next generation. Additionally, he said,

> Study after study has shown that when men make less than women, women generally don't want to marry them. Maybe they should want to marry them, but they don't. Over big populations this causes a drop in marriage, a spike in out-of-wedlock births and all the familiar disasters that inevitably follow. More drug and alcohol abuse, higher incarceration rates, fewer families formed in the next generation. This is not speculation, it's not propaganda from the evangelicals. It's social science. We know it's true. Rich people know it best of all, that's why they get married before they have kids. That model works.[52]

When we woman up

Recently, my husband and I bought a new car. The salesman said, "This is a good feature for you women—you can always find your keys. You know how women are about losing their keys."

I said to him, "Would you say that about another group? Would you say, for example, you know how Blacks are about losing their keys?" When an unflattering generalization is made about women, substitute another marginalized group into the sentence. If it doesn't work for another group, it doesn't work for women. One evening,

---

52 Benjamin Fearnow, "Fox News' Tucker Carlson: Women Refuse to Marry Men Making Less Money, Feminism Has Negative Side Effects," *Newsweek*, January 3, 2019, https://www.newsweek.com/tucker-carlson-feminism-men-vs-women-wages-marriage-fox-news-sexism-crime-1278770.

I hosted a dinner for a small group of women when we were on a cruise. A young waiter, possibly unhappy that there were no cute young *chicks* in the group, took advantage of the cultural and language difference. He served our dinners with flourishes of "a fucking delicious dish" and "Can I get you a fucking glass of wine?"

The women were highly offended, and one suggested to me, as the event organizer, that I ask my husband to handle the situation. I assured her that I, not my husband, would set the waiter straight. The waiter and I had a discussion, and from that time on, the women received respectful service throughout our cruise without the intervention of a man.

When we woman up, we find our voices to protest wrong behavior and stand up to racist and sexist jokes. We don't accept jobs we won't do or use other people as our excuse for our lack of courage. We promise not to reinforce stereotypes of women's helplessness and dependence on men. Women still face barriers of pay, equal representation in top positions, childcare, and perceptions of their value. When we know women's worth and abilities, we move forward.

CHAPTER 3

Formative Years

Now we are part of our own historical moment in time.
Our chance to control some of that narrative is in our
hands. If we don't want to be forgotten later, we must
start writing down some of our own experiences now.
—Katherine Sharp Landdeck,
The Women with Silver Wings

The stories of girls' lives compound with interest. Girls who start life on equal footing with boys often lose confidence and question their own abilities as they grow older. My personal stories of gender inequality are a series of small events, common to most women of my era. Women throughout generations have lived unaware of the institutional unfairness built into our system of laws, practices, beliefs, and behaviors because it was our everyday normal. In some cases, we recognized but felt helpless to address the problems of inequity. In others cases, we mobilized to challenge laws. This chapter looks at the norms of my time that shaped several generations of women in my life and examines the past and the progress we have made as women.

The Golden Age of Television

My growing-up years were defined by the cultural tsunami of the Golden Age of Television in the 1950s. Don't let the "golden" part fool you. This TV era was only in black and white. I considered the happiest day of my life to be the day my parents purchased a TV. Our collective lives in the United States were impacted by the template television brought.

Republican and Democratic conventions were broadcast live for the first time from Philadelphia in 1952. Americans saw Dwight Eisenhower and Adlai Stevenson debating in real time. TV introduced all of us—educated and uneducated, urban and rural, liberal and conservative—to a common perspective of personal and public norms. Three channels provided the same basic news to people of all political persuasions, resulting in a common view of the day's issues and problems. The Joe McCarthy hearings were watched by millions of people in 1954 when he alleged the conspiracy theory that Communists had infiltrated the state department and other federal government agencies. John F. Kennedy's assassination in 1963 provided TV coverage that united our country in collective grief. By 1969, forty-four million people had television sets.[53]

During the '50s decade, TV networks produced soap operas, quiz shows, comedy shows, Westerns, kid shows, and dramas. The Golden Age of Television modeled the ideal white family: cis husband as decision maker and bread winner and cis wife as cook, housekeeper, and minder of obedient children. The proper role and place for women in a perfect home was easily envisioned. *I Love Lucy* debuted in 1951. Several episodes featured Ricky spanking Lucy, his mischievous wife. No public debate followed about a man beating his wife. After all, she needed to be disciplined. *Father Knows Best* premiered in 1954, confirming men as the head of household with the ladies looking to him for wise decisions and clear thinking. *Leave It to Beaver* debuted in 1957, another all-American family TV show

---

[53] Bill Ganz, "Television," Wessels Living History Farm, 2007, https://livinghistoryfarm.org/farminginthe50s/farm-life/television/.

that featured June Cleaver cooking and vacuuming in a dress, pearls, and high heels. TV reinforced a culture that affirmed men as leaders and successful women as the "woman behind the man."

Three widely viewed adult TV shows that aired between 1951 and 1957 were *Dragnet*, a detective story; *Perry Mason*, a lawyer story; and *Gunsmoke*, a Western. The lead characters were, of course, male. Joe Friday, Perry Mason, and Matt Dillion were created based on the virtues of *real* men. They were portrayed as honest, tough, tenacious, loyal, and protectors of women and children. The male leads rarely showed emotion, and women were not necessary to finding meaning in their lives.

The women who played the supporting roles loved their male leads but, sadly, could never pull their heartstrings. We hoped that Della would win Perry Mason's affection or that Matt Dillon would drop on his knee and propose to Kitty. We even hoped that Sergeant Friday would smile. TV gave us role models of men who were above sentimentality about women and did not value their intellectual contributions. The original superheroes Superman, Batman, and Spider-Man continued the portrayal of men who were indulgent but unmoved by the amorous feelings that women had for them. Boys, as well as girls, saw expectations for their behavior and feelings defined through mass media.

My father broke the TV-man mold. He was a superhero, but he was also the first male feminist I knew. He was a hard-drinking, hard-living truck driver who could fight his way out of a bar (and sometimes did). He had a few overnights in jail. He was on the road from Monday through Friday and would come home only on the weekends. He would greet me as I jumped into his arms every Friday night and let me find mints that he had hidden in his shirt pocket.

I remember him with an apron tied around his six-foot-three-inch, large-framed body with a spatula in hand, asking if we kids would like pancakes or eggs for breakfast on Sunday morning. He cooked, cleaned, changed diapers, and played games with us all weekend. Most importantly, he expressed the words "Girls, you can be anything you want." He also lived those words. He wanted his two daughters and son to be the first in our family to go to college and pursue our dreams. He was not afraid to show emotions and told us regularly that he loved us. He believed in equality for every person.

My father was not the distant man who was so often portrayed by TV. Men like him were far and few between in the 1950s. He was a real man, strong enough to buck the male norms of the time. He had a seventh-grade education and was a poor reader, so I read the Sunday comics in the newspaper to him. He told me, "I'm real proud of the way you read, honey. I wish I could read like that."

Reading at home and in school

The majority of books we read in our 1950s elementary school had plenty of heroes but not so many she-roes. I remember my teacher saying that she would love to read *Anne of Green Gables* to the class but that boys wouldn't be interested in a book about a girl. She read *The Adventures of Tom Sawyer* instead.

Choices in our school curricula determines what we teach children and how they see themselves in the world. When groups of people are underrepresented in literature, pictures, textbooks, and history, the perceptions they hold of themselves is cast. Closing the representation gap can positively affect outcomes for females and people of racial and ethnic identities.[54] Representation of LGBTQ+ in children's literature is improving but still not the norm. Sadly, introducing children to books about LGBTQ+ has proven controversial in some school communities, and lawsuits against school districts have been filed to remove books from libraries.

Elementary school in the 1950s mirrored the beliefs about boys and girls created by the TV world. When boys misbehaved, their punishment was to sit with the girls. During recess, two boys would be chosen as team captains, and they would alternatively choose teammates one at a time. Most girls and a few humiliated boys were chosen at the end of the pack, proving what we all knew about ourselves.

---

[54] A. Adukia, A. Eble, E. Harrison, H. B. Runesha, "What We Teach About Race and Gender: Representation in Images and Text of Children's Books," *BFI Working Papers*, no. 2021–44 (July 29, 2021), https://bfi.uchicago.edu/working-paper/2021-44/.

My mom read to me as a child. We had four volumes of *Uncle Arthur's Bedtime Stories*, and each story was embedded with a moral lesson. "Nice Little Lady," a typical story from these books, stands out. Here's the story line:[55]

> Janet and a neighbor boy were playing in the dirt, and what a mess Janet was! "Faces, hands, clothes, shoes, everything—all dirty as could be."
>
> "Really, Janet," mother says, "this must stop. I want you to be a nice little lady."
>
> Shortly after, the minister's wife and her daughter pay a surprise visit to Janet's mother. Mother tells Janet to hide behind the sofa because she is so dirty that she is an embarrassment. Janet peeks out at the minister's daughter, who is clean and sitting prettily with her hands quietly folded over her lace-trimmed dress. Janet thinks, *I have never felt so dirty and ugly and ashamed of myself.*
>
> After the minister's wife leaves, Janet is allowed to come out of her hiding place. She promises "that she would stop being such a wild, rough-and-tumble little tomboy and be a nice little lady too."

This was the stuff girls were raised on. Boys got to roughhouse, drive toy trucks in dirt hills, and run around flying airplanes in the house. Girls were expected to be passive and play house with dolls. Girls who played outdoors, climbed trees, and made mud pies were called tomboys, a pejorative term at that time. Boys who loved music, cooking, or ballet were "girly boys," once again employing the greatest insult for a boy: to be compared to a girl.

According to the *Conservative Free Press* website, they provided "scientific proof that socialism is for girly men," another cheap shot

---

[55] Arthur S. Maxwell, *Uncle Arthur's Bedtime Stories* (Washington, DC: Review and Herald Publishing Company, 1924), 42–45.

about being compared to girl. They continued by wisely observing, "you probably don't need a scientific study to prove that physically weak men tend to prefer socialist policies over the heavy lifting required of a capitalist society."[56]

Around the same time that my mother was reading sexist books about nice girls to me, First Lady Mamie Eisenhower was praised in *Woman's Home Companion*, a women's magazine, being "no bluestocking feminist."[57] *Bluestocking* was a denigrating term from the eighteenth century, referring to women who had intellectual and literary interests. Even after World War II, when so many women had stepped up to the war effort, men's egos were a fragile thing that women needed to protect by not being too smart or knowledgeable.

Girls need to see themselves in literature and in media as active, competent people. The Geena Davis Institute on Gender in Media has the motto: "If she can see it, she can be it." According to its website, "This institute has amassed the largest body of research on gender prevalence in family entertainment spanning 20 years." One project analyzed the top one hundred grossing animated and non-animated family films for a ten-year period of 2007–2017. Results showed that males outnumbered female by 71 percent to 29 percent as leading characters in US family films. Female leads were less featured in action films (9 percent) and adventure films (24 percent). The good news is the trend is slowly moving upward for female representation. In 2007, 24 percent of leads were women, and by 2017, 30 percent were women.[58]

The most comprehensive study of children's books in the United States was conducted by sociologist Janice McCabe, Florida State University (FSU), in 2011. The study looked at six thousand children's books published between 1900 and 2000 and found a century of gender bias. McCabe said, "We were surprised to find that

---

56 "Finally, We Have Scientific Proof that Socialism Is for Girly Men," *Conservative Free Press*, February 25, 2019.

57 "Part II," Feminist Majority Foundation, 1953, https://feminist.org/resources/feminist-chronicles/the-feminist-chronicles-2/part-ii-1953/.

58 "The Geena Benchmark Report 2007–2017," SIE Society, February 12, 2019, https://siesociety.org/the-geena-benchmark-report-2007-2017/.

books did not become consistently more equal throughout the century." Daniel Tope, assistant professor of sociology at FSU and one of the study's coauthors, believes there is a connection between the historical ebb and flow of the women's movement and gender representation in children's books.

McCabe said,

> The widespread pattern of underrepresentation of females that we find supports the belief that female characters are less important and interesting than male characters... This may contribute to a sense of unimportance among girls and privilege among boys.[59]

A University of Chicago research project (2021) analyzed award-winning children's books. These books were selected because they were most likely to be used in schools, found in homes, and checked out of libraries. The authors of the study assert,

> Inequality of representation is a key contributor in inequality of outcomes if it instills the belief that members of the underrepresented group are inherently deficient.

The role of schools plays an important role in molding the views children hold about themselves and others. The curriculum choices made by educational experts might not be evident even to them. Across all groups, the award-winning books depicted children with lighter skin than adults. Female representation is increasing but more in pictures than in text. Latinx and Black people, especially

---

[59] Janice McCabe and Daniel Tope, "From Peter Rabbit to Curious George, FSU Study Finds 100 Years of Gender Bias in Children's Books," Florida State University, March 31, 2011, https://www.fsu.edu/news/2011/05/06/gender.bias/.

males, are underrepresented in the main collection. White males are persistently overrepresented.[60]

The books we use to teach children show them their world. How different people are portrayed and valued adds to the complexity of building children's positive identities about themselves. Since schools are heavily reliant on standardized test scores, measuring bias in curriculum has become subjective. We need to dramatically change the way we systematically measure progress in learning for children and toward eliminating bias of all kinds.

Education changes

The Cold War between the United States and the Soviet Union affected all kids growing up in the '50s. We entered the Atomic Age in this decade when both countries tested their first H-bombs. In October 1957, the Soviet Union used a ballistic missile to launch Sputnik, the first man-made satellite, into space. The Space Race was born.

Sputnik changed our educational focus almost overnight. Public perception became overwhelmingly negative about schools because the Russians were beating us. The American people blamed the schools, and schools were selected as the solution to solve the problem. Experts recommended improving science and math education programs in our elementary and secondary schools as a way to level the playing field with the Russians. Science and math rose in educational status, while the liberal arts diminished in status.

Eventually, the educational opportunities offered in math and science became the domain of boys. In her book *Girls Coming to Tech!: A History of American Engineering Education for Women*, Amy Bix, associate professor of history at Iowa State University, points out the difficult time women have had getting their feet in the door to study engineering. In the decade of the 1950s, women made up less than 1 percent of students in US engineering programs. In 2010–

---

[60] A. Adukia et al., "What We Teach About Race and Gender."

11, women earned 22 percent of the doctorates in engineering. The increase has been hard-won.

West Point was the first in the US to teach engineering, but it did not allow women to attend until 1976. Bix says that both formal and informal barriers existed to prevent women from entering this field of study. One informal barrier was that the image of engineering as a field was a man's domain. The traditions that associated engineering with masculinity has continued into the twentieth century. After WWII, women lost engineering jobs they had filled during the war. For the women who wanted to study in the engineering field, the inclusion of women was described by students, faculty, and alumni as an invasion of these programs. The feminist movement, in part, was responsible for breaking down barriers for women who wanted to study in male dominated fields.[61]

The US has seen improvement in women being accepted into engineering majors since the early days, but a significant gender gap still exists in STEM professions (science, technology, engineering, math). Women make up 28 percent of the STEM workforce, and men vastly outnumber women in STEM majors. Two of the highest-paying STEM are engineering and computer science. Women are represented by 21 percent of engineering majors and 19 percent of computer science majors. The perception continues as STEM fields are viewed as masculine.[62]

Church, women, and politics

In my homogeneous white Minnesota town, most families attended church. We had no synagogues or mosques. My understanding of heavenly concepts was that unquestioningly, God was a man. Jesus was the Son of God. Eve was made from Adam's rib, was put on earth to be his helpmate, and was blamed for Adam's fall from

---

[61] Amy Bix, *Girls Coming to Tech!: A History of American Engineering Education for Women* (2014).

[62] "The STEM Gap: Women and Girls in Science, Technology, Engineering and Mathematics," AAUW, 2019, https://www.aauw.org/resources/research/the-stem-gap/.

grace. Our prayers began, "Our Father who art in heaven" or "The Lord is my Shepherd, I shall not want." Biblical passages made clear that men held the keys to the kingdom. Woman's religious duty was to obey, be helpful, and remain silent.

When we were in seventh grade, my friend Dayna and I approached our Methodist minister and asked if we could be acolytes on Sunday morning. This activity involved wearing white robes, angelically marching down the church aisle with the congregation's admiring eyes on us, and gracefully lighting eight candles. We were nervous because girls had never been entrusted with this important role. Our minister told us that he would have to think about it and would let us know about his decision in a few days. He must have prayed, pondered, consulted church doctrine, or perhaps used common sense, but the following Sunday, Dayna and I walked down the church aisle, proving that candles could be lit by girls as well as by boys.

John Wesley, founder of the Methodist Church, was ahead of his time in his thinking about the importance of women in religion. He was one of the earliest supporters for women's participation in the church, including advocating for women's preaching and ordination. He granted a license to Sarah Crosby to preach in 1761, followed by many other licenses to women. In a particularly forceful sermon, he confronted the requirement of submissiveness from women that was the general thinking of the time by saying,

> It has long passed for a maxim with many that "women are only to be seen but not heard." And accordingly many of them are brought up in such a manner as if they were only designed for agreeable playthings! No, it is the deepest unkindness; it is horrid cruelty; it is mere Turkish barbarity, and I know not how any women of sense and spirit can submit to it.[63]

---

[63] Kenneth Cracknell and Susan J. White, *An Introductions to World Methodism* (Cambridge University Press, 2005), 217.

Even though he held women in high esteem, sadly, even Wesley could not escape his own ethnic biases. After his death in 1791, the church's inclusive views about women splintered. The United Methodist Church fractured into different denominations. The conservative United Methodist churches did not embrace Wesley's belief about the important role that women could play in the church, and today, many conservative denominations still do not allow women to be ordained or to preach.

The role for woman in the Christian church has long been a controversial issue. The King James Bible states in 1 Corinthians 11.5, "Let your women keep silence in the churches: for it is not permitted unto them to speak; but they are commanded to be under obedience, as also saith the law." This passage has been the justification for some men keeping women in secondary roles. The mayor of Wylie, Texas, requested in May 2020 that only men lead the prayers in city council meetings, citing the Bible verse quoted above to justify his request.[64] Thankfully, the Bible did not prohibit women from holding seats on city councils.

The old adage is never to talk about politics or religion. These topics raise high emotions and have little chance of changing people's minds. Historically, religion and politics have been intertwined against the backdrop of conservative and liberal religious views. Contraception, abortion, feminism, the role of women in religion, rights of LGBTQ+, and the definition of family values are a few of the issues that polarize us.

Data from the 2012 exit polls report that religious affiliation, not surprisingly, aligns with the platforms of political parties. From the study, Mormons (70 percent) are the most heavily Republican-leaning religious group in America, while the African Methodist Episcopal Church (AME) (92 percent) leans the most heavily to the left, affiliating with the Democratic party. Evangelical churches like Church of the Nazarene, Southern Baptist Convention, and

---

[64] Meredith Ysoman, "Wylie Mayor Defends Religious Belief that Only Men Should Lead Public Prayer," NBCPFW, May 20, 2020, https://www.nbcdfw.com/news/local/wylie-mayor-defends-religious-belief-that-only-men-should-lead-public-prayer/2373468/.

Lutheran Church–Missouri Synod lean to the Republican party with about 60 percent support. Mainstream churches like Presbyterian and Evangelical Lutheran Church in America tend to fall in the middle between the political parties, as do Catholics. Unitarian Universalist (70 percent) is strongly Democrat leaning. Historically, Black churches like Church of God in Christ and National Baptist Convention lean far left. Hindus, Buddhists, and Muslims also tend to lean left.[65] As Americans, we seem to find little religious common ground with those who do not share our politics.

The nexus of religion and feminism is fraught with tension. Melinda Gates says in her recent book *The Moment of Lift: How Empowering Women Changes the World,*

> As women gain rights, families flourish, and so do societies. That connection is built on a simple truth: whenever you include a group that's been excluded, you benefit everyone. And when you're working globally to include women and girls, who are half of the population, you're working to benefit all members of every community. Gender equity lifts everyone. Women's rights and society's health and wealth rise together.[66]

On June 30, 2021, Melinda French Gates pledged 2.1 billion dollars over five years from the Bill & Melinda Gates Foundation to address gender equity.

Morality, family planning, and the government

In 1952, when I was six years old, my neighbor Stevie and I had an ongoing debate about who was better, boys or girls. He supported his claim by saying boys could play baseball, drive dump trucks,

---

[65] https://www.pewresearch.org/fact-tank/2016/02/23/u-s-religious-groups-and-their-political-leanings/.

[66] Melinda Gates, *The Moment of Lift: How Empowering Women Changes the World* (Flatiron Books, 2019).

make money, and be the minister. I loved being a girl but could only offer that girls could have babies. The debate was rigged. I should never have used the baby argument. How little I knew about who controlled the rules for women and their reproductive rights. Birth control for both married and unmarried women was forbidden at the time of my feeble arguments with Stevie. Federal laws from early times set out to control women, sexuality, and family planning.

Anthony Comstock, head of the New York Society for the Suppression of Vice, was a religious fanatic who had a lasting impact on the issue of family planning and birth control in the United States. The Comstock Act of 1873, a federal law, made the distribution of any "obscene, lewd and lascivious" materials through the mail illegal. This law also made it a felony to sell, give away, or possess an obscene book, drawing, brochure, or picture. The definition of *obscene* was fuzzy, but it established that any reference to birth control was considered obscene, even if written by a physician.[67]

Comstock was designated as a special agent in the United States Post Office, where he was given the authority to arrest people who broke obscenity laws. As a part of his new role, Comstock arrested Ezra Heywood, a slavery abolitionist and advocate for women's equality. In 1878, Heywood distributed *Cupid's Yokes*, a pamphlet, where he said that women should have the right to control their own bodies. Because the pamphlet was distributed through the mail, he had broken the law. Heywood was tried, found guilty, and sentenced to two years of hard labor. His sentence was commuted by President Hayes after public pressure and protests erupted to protect free speech.[68]

Comstock also arrested doctors who were convicted of supplying written information to their patients about pregnancy and its prevention. Regardless of the law, people found ways to prevent pregnancy. They used birth control techniques like withdrawal, the rhythm method, condoms, diaphragms, contraceptive sponges,

---

[67] Brandon Burnette, "Comstock Act of 1873," *The First Amendment Encyclopedia*, https://www.mtsu.edu/first-amendment/article/1038/comstock-act-of-1873.

[68] "Birth Control Movement in the United States," *Wikipedia*.

douching, and prolonged breastfeeding. Condoms were sold in drugstores under rubber goods, and cervical caps were sold as womb protectors, thus avoiding the legal constraints.

George Bernard Shaw called the censorship "Comstockery." He went on to say that the law made the United States look like a joke in the eyes of the world. On September 24, 1996, Patricia Schroeder, former president and CEO of the Association of American Publishers, spoke to the US house of representatives in Washington, DC, about their role in reviving the Comstock Act. She referred to "Comstockery" when she said that the Telecommunications Act, passed in 1996, made it a crime to provide information on the Internet about where, how, and from whom to get an abortion. She summarized: "this body just allowed the Comstock Act to be enforced on the internet vis-à-vis anything doing with abortion."[69]

My maternal grandmother had her own unique story. She was born in 1878 and traveled from Ellis Island to North Dakota at four years old in a covered wagon. She had twelve children, her first when she was only sixteen years old. Her North Dakota farm was a rented three-bedroom house, where her children slept three in a bed with the overflow on the floor. She told me that she had no understanding of birth control, and she did not know how to keep from having children. Although her doctor told her to quit having children after her tenth pregnancy for health reasons, he would not explain how she could achieve this goal.

Her husband was a shiftless man, and my grandmother struggled to have enough food to feed a family of fourteen. She lived by the expectations of her times, knowing she had few choices. Her place was to cook, clean, care for her family, and have more babies. She suspected her life was unfair, but she was trapped by little education, her times, and the Comstock Act.

The birth control movement began in 1914, the same year my mother, the eighth of twelve children, was born. Margaret Sanger, an

---

[69] Patricia Schroeder, "Comstock Act Still on the Books," Speech to US house of representatives, Washington, DC, September 23, 1996, https://awpc.cattcenter. iastate.edu/2017/03/21/comstock-act-still-on-the-books-sept-24-1996/.

outspoken advocate of women's reproductive rights, led the movement. Sanger published and distributed eight issues of *The Woman Rebel*, a pamphlet that discussed contraception and women's health. She wanted working-class women to reject the idea that they had no control over their reproductive lives.

Sanger was arrested for violating the postal obscenity laws. She fled to England and contacted a publisher to distribute one hundred thousand copies of her pamphlet. She returned to the US to face charges when her husband, William Sanger, was arrested a year later for distributing one copy of *Family Limitation*, which promoted family planning.

Margaret and William Sanger gained sympathy from their followers when their five-year-old daughter died suddenly. The charges were dropped, but Margaret Sanger continued her advocacy for women. She was arrested again and jailed after she and her sister opened the first birth control clinic in Brooklyn with the goal of creating access for women to birth control clinics throughout the nation. She attempted to open two more birth control clinics, but both were shut down. She established the *American Birth Control League* in 1921, which later became known as *Planned Parenthood* in 1942, which today is under conservative political attack. Sanger brought the topic of birth control to our national public debate.[70]

An important birth control case, *United States v. One Package of Japanese Pessaries*, weakened the Comstock Law in 1936. Dr. Hannah Stone, a physician who specialized in gynecology, ordered a new type of diaphragm from Japan through one of Sanger's clinics. Dr. Stone was arrested and tried in this landmark case. The US Court of Appeals for the Second Circuit Court of New York affirmed that physicians had the right to distribute contraceptives to patients for medical purposes. From that point on, doctors could confer legally with their patients about family planning.[71]

---

[70] "Margaret Sanger," Morbidity and *Mortality Weekly Report*, December 3, 1999, https://www.cdc.gov/mmwr/preview/mmwrhtml/mm4847bx.htm.

[71] *United States v. One Package of Japanese Pessaries*, 86 F.2w 737 (2d Cir. 1936).

Legislating morality

During World War I, the US government had its own unique solution to fight venereal disease. As men entered the armed forces, military training camps were set up in isolated communities where the men had sexual encounters with local women, and venereal disease spread. The federal government addressed the spread of venereal disease by passing the Chamberlain-Kahn Act of 1918, later known as the American Plan.

Although the plan was written in gender neutral language, the enforcement was almost solely focused on women. Ultimately, the plan gave the government the power to quarantine any woman who was suspected of having a venereal disease. Initially, leaders supposed that prostitutes were the primary cause of sexually transmitted infections (STIs) and focused their efforts on them. A "moral zone" was set up that banned sex work within a five-mile perimeter around military training camps. Suspicious women were detained, tested, and if found to have an STI, sent to a detention center.

Leaders were surprised to learn that soldiers also contracted STIs in their hometowns, and the program was expanded to test any woman, not just prostitutes, who were suspect. By the end of the war, 15,520 prostitutes had been imprisoned. The majority never received medical hospitalization.[72]

In Sacramento, California, almost two dozen women were rounded up in one day under the umbrella of the American Plan. One woman from this roundup was Margaret Hennessey, a married woman. She was walking with her sister to the meat market when they were approached by the police morals squad and arrested because they were suspicious characters. She told police that she had a six-year-old son in school and she had to find someone to care for him.

The morals squad did not have moral concerns about her son. They took Hennessey and her sister to "Canary Cottage," where they were forcibly examined for STIs. If the sisters had been found to have

---

[72] "Chamberlain-Kahn Act," *Wikipedia*.

had venereal diseases, they would have been sent to a penal institution. They were disease-free and summarily released.

Of the twenty-two women who were rounded up, one was eventually arrested. Records show that detained women who were believed to be immoral had no due process and lived difficult lives. Medical treatment included being forced to ingest mercury and arsenic. Shockingly, the American Plan continued until 1970 in some states. By then, as many as one hundred thousand women may have been forcibly tested, but records are incomplete.[73]

Germany provided brothels for its soldiers, the French legalized prostitution and provided condoms, and Britain provided condoms and allowed their solders to visit brothels. The strategy of the Americans was to put commanding officers in charge of their soldiers' sexual health. Thousands of American troops arrived in France in 1918, and they were ordered to use purity and chastity as their birth control method. French prostitutes were maligned by the US Federal Government through posters, ads, and lectures by chaplains. Not until after the war did statistics show that the French women were less dangerous than American women in spreading venereal disease.[74] In France, where prostitution was legal, regulations were put in place, including being checked regularly by doctors.

Women's reproductive rights have generally been at the mercy of men. The first reported artificial insemination by donor (AID) was performed by Dr. William H. Pancoast in 1884. He anesthetized his patient with chloroform, and without her knowledge, impregnate her with a rubber syringe using sperm from the best-looking student in his class. Six medical students witnessed the procedure. Twenty-

[73] Scott Stern, *The Trials of Nina McCall: Sex, Surveillance, and the Decades-Long Government Plan to Imprison "Promiscuous" Women* (Beacon Press, 2018).

[74] Scott W. Stern, "America's Forgotten Mass Imprisonment of Women Believed to Be Sexually Immoral," *History*, March, 27 2019, https://www.madinamerica.com/2019/04/americas-forgotten-mass-imprisonment-women-believed-sexually-immoral/.

five years later, the impregnation was reported in a medical journal by one of the students who had been present.[75]

In 1954, the Superior Court of Cook County, Illinois, heard *Doornbos v. Doornbos*, an "artificial insemination by donor" case. A husband sought a divorce on the grounds of his wife's adultery. She had submitted to AID with the express consent of her husband. The *Doornbos v. Doornbos* ruling follows:

> Homologous Artificial Insemination (when the specimen of semen used is obtained from the husband of the woman) is not contrary to public policy and good morals, and does not present any difficulty from the legal point of view. Heterologous Artificial Insemination (when the specimen of semen used is obtained from a third party or donor) with or without the consent of the husband is contrary to public policy and good morals, and constitutes adultery on the part of the mother. A child so conceived is not a child born in wedlock and therefore is illegitimate. As such, it is the child of the mother, and the father has no right or interest in said child.[76]

Artificial insemination by donor, *even with* the husband's consent, was ruled to be adultery on the part of the woman, and the child was ruled to be a bastard. The divorce was granted. An American court, for the first time, took a definite stand on legal issues involving artificial insemination.

The decade of the 1960s brought sweeping change and conflicting messages about the use of birth control. In 1960, the birth control method known as the pill was approved by the FDA. Three years after the development of the pill, Pope Paul VI issued his encyc-

---

[75] "Letter to the Editor: Artificial Impregnation," *The Medical World*, April 1909, 163–164.

[76] *Doornbos v. Doornbos* (1954) No. 54 S.14981, Super. Ct., Cook County, Ill.

lical *Humanae vitae* (Of Human Life), which stated that every use of artificial contraceptives was immoral. The Catholic Church was one of the largest individual denominations in the United States, and many members felt compelled to comply to the authority of the Pope.

In 1965, the Supreme Court gave married couples the right to use birth control in *Griswold v. Connecticut*, ruling that the right to privacy was protected in the Constitution. This ruling marked the end of enforcing the Comstock Act of 1873, although it has never been repealed and remains on the books. Mainstream Protestants and Jews readily used the pill as a legitimate family planning aid, while evangelicals and Catholics mostly avoided its use. When I was pregnant with my second child in 1972, the Supreme Court ruled in *Eisenstadt v. Baird* that birth control was legal for *all* people, both married or unmarried. In 1973, in *Roe v. Wade*, the Supreme Court ruled that abortion was legal. Women's modern reproductive world changed dramatically. Women had choices about family planning, careers, educational opportunities, and their own sexuality.

The availability of the pill, *Eisenstadt v. Baird* and *Roe v. Wade* fueled the sexual revolution, which caused greater concern and anguish about feminism. Anti-feminists saw the changes in law and medicine as harmful encroachments on family values. Evangelical radio host and author Nancy Leigh DeMoss (also known as Nancy DeMoss Wolgemuth) condemned birth control and feminism in her 2001 book *Lies Women Believe*. She said female selfishness leads…

> To the legitimization and promotion of such practices as contraception, sterilization, and family planning. As a result, unwittingly, millions of Christian women and couples have helped further Satan's attempt to limit human reproduction and thereby destroy life.[77]

---

[77] Tara Isabella Burton, "How Birth Control Became Part of the Evangelical Agenda," *Vox*, October 7, 2017, https://www.vox.com/identities/2017/10/7/16259952/birth-control-evangelical-agenda.

Conclusion

The decade of the 1950s seems like a long time ago. Seventy years later, the same issues divide us. In the decade of the 2020s, TV offers dramatically differing views that reflect what Americans should stand for, orbiting around the politics of conservative and progressives. Russia is still in play with questions about their interference in our 2016 election, aggression toward other countries, the killing of a journalist in American, and 2021 cyberattacks. We have become more critical of our education system and still believe that standardized tests best inform us about the success of students and schools.

Church and politics remain entangled and fraught with dissension. The Methodist Church will vote in 2022 whether to split into a conservative United Methodist Church and a liberal United Methodist Church. At the heart of the issue is whether to embrace the full inclusion of people of all gender expressions and sexual identities. The Roman Catholic bishops of the United States overwhelmingly voted on June 18, 2021, to draft guidelines that would deny President Biden, a devout Catholic, the right to the sacrament because of his support for abortion.[78]

Abortion and birth control remain hot buttons between conservatives and liberals. Scott Lloyd, former director of Refugee Resettlement at the US Department of Health and Human Services and a conservative Christian, stated that "to oppose abortion, the pro-life movement should speak with a unified voice in opposition to contraception as well [as to abortion]."[79] Scott was removed from office in November 2018 after allegations of interfering with the reproductive rights of refugees.

Individual states are creating abortion laws that take decision-making away from women, their families, and their faith and beliefs. Parents may feel they are not able to support a child, or they

---

[78] Elizabeth Diaz, "Targeting Joe Biden, Catholic Bishops Advance Controversial Communion Plan," *The New York Times*, June 18, 2018, https://www.nytimes.com/2021/06/18/us/targeting-biden-catholic-bishops-advance-controversial-communion-plan.html.

[79] *National Catholic Bioethics Quarterly* 15, no. 2: 231–239.

may wish not to have one. If the time comes when the government decides families have no say about the children they bring into the world, then the government must be responsible for supporting families with childcare, food, health care, education, housing, and clothing.

Sister Joan Chittister, Benedictine nun and activist, said in 2004,

> I do not believe that just because you're opposed to abortion, that that makes you pro-life. In fact, I think in many cases your morality is deeply lacking if all you want is a child born but not a child fed, not a child educated, not a child housed. And why would I think that you don't? Because you don't want any tax money to go there. That's not pro-life. That's pro-birth.[80]

Companies can be exempted from providing insurance coverage for birth control, based on managements' religious or moral grounds. The Supreme Court ruled (5–4) in *Burwell v. Hobby Lobby Stores Inc.* on March 25, 2014, that requiring employers to provide insurance to their female employees with no-cost access to contraception violated the Religious Freedom Restoration Act. Claire McCaskill, former US senator from Missouri, tweeted on June 25, 2021,

> Update: MO Republican men in Jeff City spent yesterday trying to figure out how IUDs work and labeling all women that have them as having abortions.

How do we learn? What questions should we ask? Why do we find ourselves full circle with the same issues as seventy years ago?

---

[80] Heidi Schlumpf, "Sr. Joan Chittister's 2004 quote on 'pro-life' versus 'pro-birth' goes viral," *National Catholic Reporter*, May 23, 2019, https://www.ncronline.org/news/politics/sr-joan-chittisters-2004-quote-pro-life-versus-pro-birth-gocs-viral.

Women can lead the way. We who have lived this journey can confront the language, actions, norms, and the outcomes of sexism. We can vote, use our voice, and extend the invitation for others to join us in creating a new sensitivity and inclusivity for all people.

CHAPTER 4

A Turn for Women

And to all the little girls who are watching this, never doubt that
you are valuable, powerful, and deserving of every chance and
opportunity in the world to pursue and achieve your dreams.
                              —Hillary Clinton, Presidential Concession
                                        Speech, November 9, 2016

The decade of the 1960s was a time of hope and heartbreak. It
opened with the election of President John F. Kennedy. That same
year, the US sent 3,500 troops to Vietnam, which created disillusionment with government that became embedded in our collective
consciousness. Martin Luther King Jr. brought us the power of the
vision of equality in his "I Have a Dream" speech in August 1963.
Three months later, President Kennedy was assassinated. Dr. King's
assassination followed in 1968. Our thinking about social justice and
civil rights was profoundly affected, setting the stage for the Civil
Rights Movement.

The decade evolved into bitter polarization between young and
old, conservative and liberal. Woodstock—famous for hippies, drugs,
sex, and anti-establishment thinking—sent the message that young
Americans were members of the counterculture movement, rejecting
the commonly held views and values of equity and fairness. They
pledged to take on the challenges of stopping the Vietnam War, ending poverty, addressing racial segregation, discovering solutions to

environmental pollution, and finding a way to live together in peace. A sense that America was forever changed pervaded the country.

The 1960s vibrated with energy and innovation, discord and disillusionment. The Beatles released their first single "Love Me Do," construction began on the Berlin Wall, and the peace corps was established. Rachel Carson's book *Silent Spring* (1961) warned of irreparable harm to life on Earth due to man-made pollution and lethal chemicals produced by industries. Advances in technology soared. The US put a man on the moon, the first human heart transplant was performed in South Africa, and the first handheld calculator was invented by Texas Instruments at a cost of 2,500 dollars each. Bob Dylan aptly summed up the mood in American in his song "The Times They Are a-Changin'" (1964).

Gloria Steinem and Betty Friedan introduced an era of feminist activism that focused the spotlight on women's rights and the institutional inequality built into our laws and everyday practices. The word *feminist* began being used in general conversations, and everyone had an opinion on the issues of women's rights. Bella Abzug and Shirley Chisholm joined with feminists to open the eyes of America to the restrictions that women faced. Women were about to have their turn. Male privilege was under attack.

Civil rights in 1964

I began my college career at the University of Minnesota, the same year Congress passed the Civil Rights Act of 1964, which was signed into law by President Lyndon Johnson. The Civil Rights Act was focused on ending discrimination in many areas of American life. It listed the prohibited areas of discrimination in schools, public places, and employment and detailed the reasons people could not be discriminated against: race, religion, color, or national origin. No mention was made of discrimination based on sex.

The Civil Rights Act was divided into various titles: Title II, for example, addressed discrimination in public accommodations; Title IV addressed the desegregation of public schools; and Title VI prohibited discrimination by recipients of federal funds on the basis of race, color, and national origin. Two days before the act was about to be voted on, Congressman Howard Smith, Virginia, made a last-minute amendment to Title VII. He added *sex* to the list of banned discriminatory practices: race, religion, color, sex, or national origin.

Smith was strongly opposed to the Civil Rights Act and had quashed similar legislation earlier. Many historians believe his late addition of the word *sex* was an unsuccessful effort by the Congressman to derail the passage of the entire act. His strategy backfired, the law passed and went into effect July 1965, and *sex* was added as a legitimate area where discrimination was banned.

While the national dialogue about women's rights was gaining steam in 1964–65, I lived in a large on-campus, women-only dormitory at the University of Minnesota, where the temperature frequently dipped below zero. We freshwomen dorm residents were required to wear dresses and nylons for our dorm dinner, which was served cafeteria style. Usually we rushed back from classes in freezing weather and then changed into ladylike clothes. A female monitor sat at the beginning of the serving line and touched our legs to make sure we were wearing nylons, which to be clear, involved wearing a girdle or garter belt—no pull-up nylons at that time.

The retelling of this story now sounds a little creepy. We rebelled to this nonsense by wearing nylons with so many snags and holes that our legs looked wooly. We had curfews and faced punishment if we came into the dorm at night even five minutes late. Men had few rules, and although women complained, we were, in the end, compliant.

The next year, in 1965, President Johnson issued Executive Order 11246 to begin developing regulations for ensuring compliance with the Civil Rights Act. Discrimination based on sex was again absent from this order. President Johnson gave a special message to Congress in 1967 on "Equal Justice," where he talked about the need to expand the areas covered by the 1964 Act. He talked solely about racial discrimination and again omitted any reference to sexual discrimination.

The Equal Employment Opportunity Commission (EEOC) was formed to implement Title VII. Their decision not to enforce equal rights for women gave rise to The National Organization for Women (NOW) in 1966. NOW's purpose was to give voice to the repeated omission of sex discrimination and protections for woman in the Civil Rights Act. NOW elected officers that included Betty Friedan, president, and Richard Graham, vice president. The organization set up seven task forces to address: women's employment, education, poverty, legal and political rights, family, image, and religion. NOW was the first to endorse the legalization of abortion, and they were recognized as a driving force for women and a formidable force for women's rights.

In 1964, high school girls were not allowed to play organized sports, although a handful of girls were cheerleaders for boys' sports. The place of girls in sports was rooted in nineteenth century thinking. Physical activity was thought to be hazardous to women. The onset of menstruation was believed to weaken women. Men advised women to curtail their muscular and intellectual labors in order to preserve the finite amount of energy granted to them in their lifetime. If women wanted to be involved in physical activities, they chose noncompetitive activities that were deemed appropriate for women, such as walking, gardening, tennis, archery, croquet, and horseback riding.

In my senior year of high school, 1964, there still were no girls' varsity sports in schools. Those girls who wanted to play basketball did so wearing our green gym suits in an after-school program called GAA (Girls Athletic Association). There were no refs, no coaches, and no resources, and we played by girls' basketball rules. We could only bounce the ball three times, and then we were required to pass it. Harkening back to the 1890s, we were not allowed to cross the center line of the basketball court because too much running might fatigue us. One robust girl on each team was appointed a rover. This girl could run full court. How frustrating for the rest of the girls who stood on one side of the court and watched without being able to join in. On the weekend, girls in my neighborhood played pickup basketball and baseball with the neighborhood boys, using boys' rules. In many cases, we girls were better than the boys, and we were not overly fatigued by the physical effort.

Women in college played intramural sports against other clubs within the school, and men played intercollegiate sports against teams from other colleges. Women athletes received no recognition, support, or resources. Men won trophies, scholarships, championships, and endorsements.

While girls were bouncing the ball three times and playing half-court basketball, two women, "Babe" Didrikson Zaharias and Althea Gibson, showed what women could do in sports. Zaharias was named "Woman Athlete of the Half Century" in 1950 for her skills in basketball, baseball, track-and-field, and golf. She won two gold medals in the 1932 Summer Olympics and ten LPGA championships. She is regarded as one of the greatest athletes of all times.

Althea Gibson, a gifted tennis player, found most tennis tournaments closed to African Americans in the 1940s and 1950s. Her undeniable skill challenged the rules. She went on to play in major tennis events and was the first African American to win a tennis Grand Slam title by winning the French Championships in singles and doubles, Wimbledon, and the US Nationals in one year. She was voted "Female Athlete of the Year" by the associated press in both 1956 and 1958.

In one respect, Zaharias and Gibson were like all women of their era: they were not allowed to play sports in school. Even though they likely demonstrated greater athletic ability than their male classmates, the same opportunities were not available to girls from elementary school through college.

The Civil Rights Act of 1964, the Voting Right Act of 1965, and the Equal Rights Amendment (ERA) expanded the promise of civil rights for Blacks and women. A growing social consciousness in our country began accepting differences in people and in lifestyle choices. There was a conservative backlash to President Johnson's Great Society initiatives. Conservative forces gained power as the South became solidly Republican after a generation of voting for Democrats. Republican Richard Milhous Nixon was elected President in 1969, marking a change in direction for the country.

The decade of the 70s

The 1970s decade was a turning point for American women and an era of change for Americans. The decade opened with the Women's Strike for Equality protest, marking the fiftieth anniversary of the ratification of the Nineteenth Amendment, which gave women the right to vote. Title IX changed women's access to opportunities never before available. The Education of All Handicapped Children Act (PL 94-142) (1975) guaranteed a free appropriate public education to each child with a disability. The Supreme Court gave women the right to an abortion in *Roe v. Wade*, and the ERA (Equal Rights Amendment) was a passionate goal for women across the country.

As feminism grew globally, the 1970s saw women take their places as world leaders. Women served as prime ministers of their countries: Margaret Thatcher, UK; Golda Meir, Israel; Elisabeth Domitien, Central African Republic; and Indira Gandhi, India. In the United States, the proportion of women holding seats in Congress tripled. While women took their turn at sports and leadership, progress in other areas of equity stalled or was adversely affected.

Newly elected president Nixon was a champion for women and a strong supporter of the Equal Rights Amendment. Daniel Patrick Moynihan, Nixon's urban affairs director, wrote a memo to White House staff in 1970, where he predicted, "Female equality will be a major cultural/political force of the 1970s. The essential fact is that we have educated women for equality, but have not really given it to them."[81]

Nixon said in his 1972 State of the Union address, "While every woman may not want to have a career outside the home, every woman should have the freedom to choose whatever career she wishes, and an equal chance to pursue it." He made a historic number of appointments of women to important positions in the federal government and appointed the Task Force on Women's Rights and Responsibilities to write a report on how to improve women's status in the US.

---

[81]   Daniel Patrick Moynihan, memo to White House staff, August 20, 1969.

Simple rights for women were slow to come. When my husband and I were newly married in 1968, we needed to buy a washing machine. We applied for a Sears credit card. Our application was rejected. The reason given was that my income was not considered in the application, even though it exceeded that of my husband's. Women did not have access to credit cards. Fairness prevailed. Progressive people advocated for the Equal Credit Opportunity Act (ECOA), which was passed into law in October 1974, the year Nixon left office in disgrace. This Act made it unlawful to discriminate with respect to any aspect of a credit transaction on the basis of sex or marital status. The act was amended in 1976 to include race, religion, ethnicity, and other areas. Too late for that washing machine we needed to buy in 1968 but a step forward for women.

Title IX: women's turn: the 1970s

In 1972, four years after I graduated from college, President Nixon signed into law a landmark piece of legislation: Title IX of the Educational Amendments of 1972 (20 USC. 1681 24 seq.). The main purpose was to prohibit discrimination on the basis of sex in educational programs receiving federal funding from elementary school through college. The sleeping giant of opportunities for women was poked.

During my undergraduate years from 1964–68, sports were not the only area that barred women from participation. Another example was the University of Minnesota Marching Band, which, like all Big Ten University Marching Bands, banned women. Under Title IX, women could no longer be barred from being police officers, firefighters, FBI agents, or marching in university bands. The University of Minnesota admitted its first female to the marching band in 1972. In 2006 the University of Minnesota had its first female drum major, and in 2016, Betsy McCann became the first female marching band director in the Big Ten. Forty-five years later, I watched my granddaughter march onto the University of Illinois football field in her band uniform, playing her clarinet. I thought to myself, *What was all the fuss about?*

Senators Jesse Helms, Paul Laxalt, Carl T. Curtis, and Paul Fannin, among others, condemned Title IX in its entirety. Various amendments to the bill were submitted, including one by Senator Jesse Helms, which said athletic activities were not a required part of schools' curriculum, and therefore, Title IX should not be applied to athletics. The NCAA (National Collegiate Athletic Association) and the college football coaches strongly opposed Title IX.

The NCAA filed a lawsuit in February 1976 to challenge its legality, which was dismissed. Repeated attempts to repeal or amend Title IX went all the way to the Supreme Court. In 1987, the Civil Rights Restoration Act (CRRA) established that *all* programs and activities in educational institutions must be open to women, not just the specific programs that received federal funding. The act was passed over President Reagan's veto. Challenges and modifications to Title IX have continued almost every year since then.

Title IX continues to change, evolve, and be challenged. May 6, 2020, Betsy de Vos, secretary of education under President Donald Trump, added a controversial two-thousand-page rule to Title IX. This rule governs how schools receiving federal funding must handle sexual misconduct allegations for seventy-six million kindergarten through college students. Proponents of the rule said that it increases fairness for those who have been accused of sexual misconduct. Opponents argued that the rule gives more protections to abusers in a system that is already set up in their favor. They claimed the narrowed definition of sexual harassment will mean victims must be harassed multiple times before they can file complaints. The rule took effect August 14, 2020.[82]

The Biden administration has begun the process to undo the Trump-era Title IX rules. In March 2021, President Joe Biden released Executive Order 13988: Preventing and Combating Discrimination of the Basis of Gender Identity or Sexual Orientation. This EO reverses Trump-era policies that removed protection for transgen-

---

[82] Alanna Vagianos, "Betsy DeVos's Campaign to Roll Back Sexual Assault Survivor Rights Is Complete," *HuffPost*, May 6, 2020, https://www.huffpost.com/entry/betsy-devos-rolls-back-sexual-assault-survivor-rights-title-ix_n_5eb31baa c5b6e74a713919c5.

dered students, and it expands Title IX of the Education Amendments of 1972. Democrats and civil rights groups praised the order, saying that all students deserve the protection of being free from discrimination. Republicans and critics of the order said that girls' sports will be destroyed. Other Republican lawmakers are looking for ways for their states to circumvent the order.

The effects of Title IX

While Title IX is best known for opening doors for women's athletics, it affected all other areas of education for girls, such as women winning college scholarships and the right of pregnant students to continue their education. Now women earn nearly half of medical degrees, compared to only 9 percent in 1972. A few years after Title IX was signed into law, educators created the first Women's History Week to help schools comply with Title IX rules.

Until 1972, policy makers thought girls simply were not interested in sports. Prior to Title IX, only 295,000 girls participated in primary and secondary school sports compared to 3.67 million boys. Forty-five years later, in 2017, 3.42 million girls were competing in high school sports compared to 4.57 million boys.[83]

By 1980, gender stereotypes of masculine tomboys playing sports were replaced by all kinds of girls handling the basketball and swinging a bat. The struggle was hard, even with support of the law. When women were finally allowed to play high school and collegiate sports, women teachers were called upon to coach, even though many had no knowledge of the sport to which they were assigned. Practice times for women's sports were those that men teams didn't want, and varsity competition times were the ones best for men, their coaches, and the revenue stream. The majority of funding still went for boys' sports. Girls got the leftovers. The increase in women's ath-

---

[83] "High School Sports Participation Increases for 29th Consecutive Year," National Federation of High Schools, September 11, 2018, https://www.nfhs.org/articles/high-school-sports-participation-increases-for-29th-consecutive-year/.

letics has come about despite persistent underinvestment in women's athletic programs in schools and universities.

At Northern Illinois University, like many universities in the United States, women, illogically, did not get varsity letters when they played varsity sports. February 2019 NIU called back their female athletes to recognize women who should have been awarded a varsity letter prior to 1982. At the collegiate level, women's varsity sports increased by 600 percent forty years after Title IX was passed. With this surge, women gained more access to higher education and benefitted from women's athletic scholarships.[84]

Stephen Moore should have been less cavalier about the power of women and sports. President Trump nominated him to the Federal Reserve Board of Governors in 2019. First, Moore proposed women should not participate in March Madness tournaments. In March 2019, he wrote, "Here's the change I propose: No more women refs, no women announcers, no women beer venders, no women anything."

He went further to say he'd make an exception if they looked like Bonnie Bernstein (CBS sports journalist). He added that she knew nothing about basketball but suggested she could wear a halter top. He said that to see a woman ref a men's NCAA game was an obscenity and that liberals celebrate these gains as a triumph for gender equity. He complained about equal pay for women in tennis and ended by saying, "I hate women's basketball."

Later, when faced with a nomination for the Federal reserve, he said he had a sense of humor and was just spoofing. His jokes were not funny to women, who were no longer powerless. He withdrew his nomination after public pressure over his sexist statements. Women found their voice and answered him.[85]

The NCAA has faced sharp criticism. In 2021, Sedona Prince shared a tweet that caught the attention of sports fans when she

[84] Ibid.
[85] Andrew Kaczynski and Paul LeBlanc, "Trump Fed Pick Stephen Moore Called It a 'Travesty' that Women 'Feel Free' to Play Sports with Men," CNN, April 22, 2019, https://www.cnn.com/2019/04/22/politics/stephen-moore-federal-reserve-kfile/index.html.

showed the difference between the NCAA men's and women's basketball teams' facilities for weight lifting equipment. An external gender equity review was released in August, 2021. It said, "The NCAA has not lived up to its stated commitment to diversity, inclusion and gender equity among its student-athletes, coaches and administrators."[86] Among changes for 2022, the NCAA will use March Madness branding for both men's and women's tournaments, and funding equity for the tournaments will be changed.

Downturn for women

Other battles continue to be waged against women. As a child, I wondered about my mother's harsh views of men. She had intensely negative feelings about her father. When we were adults, my mother confided to my sister and me that her father had sexually abused her. In her era, as sometimes today, victims of abuse remained silent about the nightmares they survived.

A 2019 federal study report estimates that one in sixteen (equivalent to 3.3 million) women's first experience with sexual intercourse was forced. Subsequently, these women are at greater risk for long-term health issues like unwanted pregnancies, gynecological and general health issues. Often, they risk social censure. The average age of a woman at the time of involuntary intercourse was fifteen and a half years. The assailants' average age was twenty-seven.[87]

In October 2018, New Jersey family court judge John F. Russo Jr. asked a woman who was alleging a sexual attack if she had tried closing her legs to prevent intercourse. The New Jersey State Supreme Court's Advisory Committee on Judicial Conduct was unanimous

---

[86] Dean Golembeski, "NCAA's March Madness Brand to Include Women in 2022 Basketball Tournament," *Best Colleges*, September 30, 2021, https://www.bestcolleges.com/news/2021/09/30/ncaa-march-madness-women-basketball-tournament-final-four/.

[87] Rita Giordano, "One in 16 U.S. Women's First Sexual Experience Was Forced, New Study Finds," *The Philadelphia Inquirer*, September 19, 2019, https://www.inquirer.com/health/rape-girls-first-intercourse-forced-sexual-experience-assault-young-trauma-20190916.html.

in its decision to recommend Judge Russo be suspended for three months without pay, citing emotional immaturity. As often happens, victims are revictimized by those who believe that women who are sexually attacked were "asking for it" or believe that women could have prevented the abuse had they tried harder. Some misguided people suggest that women actually enjoyed the assault. On January 28, 2020, the Supreme Court of New Jersey filed a formal complaint to remove John Russo Jr. from office.[88] Victim shaming is alive and well in America.

Crime and punishment

When we were young, my neighbor Stevie and I were involved in a crime spree. I convinced Stevie to help me disarm ten animal steel jaw traps that had been set out in a nearby field. Next, we carried the traps to the river and threw them in, believing we had heroically saved dozens of animals' lives. Later that day, police arrived at my house. They reported that Stevie and I had been seen near the river where the stolen traps had been disposed. The police explained that Stevie would be punished, but I was off the hook. Everyone knew a girl would not do something like that, and she must have been following a boy's directions.

Times for women associated with crime have changed, and not in a good way. The divorce rate increased in the 1970s, and more women became single heads of household, spiraled into poverty, became addicted to drugs, suffered mental health issues, became homeless, and were incarcerated. Women became the fastest-growing group in American prisons and jails, increasing fourteenfold from 1970 to 2014.[89]

Nixon was a paradox. His support of women's rights broke ground. Then his punitive side emerged when he responded to the Woodstock rebellion of antiwar youth. Shortly after taking office,

---

[88] "In the Matter of John F. Russo, Jr.," Supreme Court of New Jersey Decisions, 2020.

[89] Robert Valencia, "Incarcerated Women, the Fastest-Growing Population Behind Bars, Face Unique Challenges," *Newsweek*, October, 20 2017.

he declared a "war on drugs" and called drug abuse public enemy number one. To combat the public enemy, federal drug control agencies increased in size, and policies like mandatory sentencing and no-knock warrants were put in place.

Following Nixon's lead, New York governor Nelson Rockefeller promoted drug laws that resulted in life sentences, no parole, and no plea bargaining—even for juveniles. Other states followed his lead. President Ronald Reagan's eight-year term saw an explosion in the prison population from 329,000 in 1980 to 627,000 in 1988.[90] The federal government passed the 1986 Anti-Drug Abuse Act with goals of attaining a drug-free America and reestablishing the death penalty. Incarceration became a national solution to drug issues, with little attention given to underlying causes or treatment.

Woman and Blacks were disproportionally affected, and the data is surprising. Between 1980 and 2017, the number of incarcerated women increased by an astonishing 750 percent, rising from 23,378 to 225,060 inmates. In 2018, 4 percent of females in the world lived in the US, yet the US accounted for 33 percent of world's female prison population. Between 2000 to 2019, the rate of African American women in state and federal prisons declined by 55 percent, while that of white women increased by 44 percent, and Latinx women increased by 5 percent. However, Black women remain the largest number of incarcerated women, and even though white women are the fastest-growing group, it will be years before their cohort is larger than Black women.[91]

The increase of women in prison added to overcrowded conditions. Expansion of for-profit prisons led to the US prison-industrial complex, where private prisons have become a mainstay in our country. Critics assert that when profit became the focus of prisons, corners were cut, and greater numbers of prisoners were needed for better profit margins. The increase of women in prisons helped achieve

---

[90] James Cullen, "The History of Mass Incarceration," Brennan Center for Justice, July 20, 2018, https://www.brennancenter.org/our-work/analysis-opinion/history-mass-incarceration.

[91] "Incarcerated Women and Girls," The Sentencing Project, https://www.sentencingproject.org/publications/incarcerated-women-and-girls/.

the primary goal of profit. Prisons were not designed for women. Few prisons consider female needs including pregnancy, neonatal care, separation from children, gynecological care, menstrual hygiene, as well as the need for female guards and security. When women are released from prison, they are ill prepared to take their places as productive citizens.

Angela Davis and Cassandra Shaylor stated,

> Women prisoners represent one of the most disenfranchised and invisible adult populations in our society. The absolute power and control the state exercises over their lives both stems from and perpetuates the patriarchal and racist structures that, for centuries, have resulted in the social domination of women.[92]

Prison reform, especially for women, needs to focus on more productive and less punitive ways to address the issues that end in incarceration.

Women have pushed forward slowly against the walls of societal resistance. Today, my granddaughters have credit cards in their own names (maybe too many). They can play sports in school and can teach when they are pregnant. When they interview for jobs, they cannot be asked when they plan to have children, and they cannot be fired because they are pregnant. They can work at jobs that were once reserved only for men. While women are still underrepresented in top positions, they continue to move upward.

Every rejection, denial, and challenge because of my gender also hurt my husband. He did not get the credit card we needed, the raise from my promotion, and in some cases, a contented wife. Women's issues are everybody's issues. There are no challenges that women face that do not impact men. We are not finished with equity work. We

---

[92] Angela Y. Davis and Cassandra Shaylor, "Gender and the Prison Industrial Complex California and Beyond," *Meridians: Feminism, Race, Transnationalism* 2, no. 1 (November 17, 2001): 1–25.

will continue to advocate until the scales of Lady Justice are balanced among all people. Our language, our behavior, and our actions must reflect who we are as Americans, what we teach our children, and for what we stand. When we woman up, we thank all those who have fought for equal rights, celebrate the people who stand with us, and continue to work for laws of equality, equity, and justice for all people.

CHAPTER 5

The Science of Being a Woman

> To prove women's inferiority, antifeminists began to draw
> not only, as before, on religion, philosophy and theology,
> but also on science: biology, psychology and so forth.
> —Simone de Beauvoir, *The Second Sex*

Congratulations to three women: Dr. Emmanuelle Charpentier and Dr. Jennifer A. Doudna, who were jointly awarded the 2020 Nobel Prizes in Chemistry for the development of a method of genome editing, and Dr. Andrea Ghez, in Physics for discoveries about black holes. We've come a long way from the time when men conducted scientific research about women in the eighteenth and nineteenth centuries. The biases men held reinforced faulty assumptions and confirmed what men wanted to believe about women's inferiority. The results embedded stereotypes and myths about women that have been perpetuated to this day. Even though science is regarded as truth, confirmation bias is a danger that exists in all research studies. In the case of women, men collected and interpreted *evidence* that verified their biases even when faced by common sense and patterns of observation that told a different story.

In the beginning, the theory of evolution

In school, we learned Charles Darwin was a renowned scientist and a good guy who advanced our understanding of how the natural world works. Darwin's scientific theories about women's abilities were widely accepted in the nineteenth century. Known for his theory of evolution by natural selection, he explained that the best adapted plants and animals flourish and pass their traits to the next generation, while weaker plants and animals are poorly adapted to their environment and will not survive or reproduce. What we did not learn in school was that Darwin's theory of evolution was racist and sexist. Darwin and other scientists embedded a view of women into our country's collective thinking from which there has been a slow recovery.

At the core of Darwin's theory of evolution was that women were less evolved than men and, therefore, biologically inferior. In his book *The Descent of Man and Selection in Relation to Sex*, Darwin wrote,

> The chief distinction in the intellectual powers of the two sexes is shewn by man attaining to a higher eminence, in whatever he takes up, than woman can attain—whether requiring deep thought, reason, imagination, or merely the use of the senses and hands... Thus, man has ultimately become superior to woman.[93]

As a preeminent scientist of his day, Darwin had much to consider about how he would spend his life and time. In 1838, the ever-practical Darwin was pondering marriage, and consequently, he drew up a list of the pros and cons of marriage. He noted the advantages of marriage were having a constant companion and friend in old age who will feel interest in one, having an object to be beloved and

---

[93] Charles Darwin, *The Descent of Man, and Selection in Relation to Sex* (London: John Murray, 1871), 2:327.

played with, something better than a dog, someone to take care of the house, the charms of female chitchat, and good for one's health.

The disadvantages of marriage included losing the freedom to go where one liked, not having the conversation of clever men at clubs, being forced to visit relatives and to bend in every trifle, perhaps quarrelling, not being able to read in the evenings, and ultimately, a terrible loss of time.[94] Darwin decided that the pros outweighed the cons, and he opted for marriage.

Of interest, in 1837, Darwin was working on his theory of transmutation of species, the concept where one species turns into another through evolution, when he asked his first cousin Emma Westwood to be his wife. Francis Galton, Darwin's half cousin (of whom you will hear more), warned Darwin about the potential dangers of inbreeding. Charles Darwin and Emma Westwood married in 1839. They had ten children, three of whom died in infancy and several others who had serious health issues.

Emma was a religious woman who questioned, read, and thought deeply about her faith, while at the same time, Charles was losing his faith. She was concerned that their different beliefs would separate them, so she and Darwin decided to be completely open with each other about their individual views, including scientific theories and Christianity.

Darwin's first book, *The Voyage of the Beagle*, 1839, was an account of a five-year expedition where he began developing his theory of evolution of species by natural selection. He published *On the Origin of Species* in 1859 and *The Descent of Man, and Selection in Relation to Sex* in 1871. Darwin pondered whether he should publish his new theory of evolutionary biology because he knew it would be controversial in a Christian nation where the Bible explained creation through the story of Adam and Eve. Eventually, he did publish this theory and found his concern was not underestimated. Controversy and criticism surfaced immediately, pitting Christian dogma against

---

[94] *The Correspondence of Charles Darwin, Volume 2: 1837–1843* (Cambridge University Press).

evolutionary theories. These tensions continue to divide our politics and religious beliefs to this day.

Antoinette Blackwell was one of the first women to criticize Darwin's conclusions that women were inferior to men as a result of nature. Darwin opined that because man used weapons and tools throughout the ages, he had ultimately become superior to woman. In response to Darwin, Blackwell published *The Sexes Throughout Nature* (1875), where she argued for a healthful equilibrium of the sexes. She believed that Darwin's theories set the stage for defrauded womanhood.[95]

Her criticisms went unheeded. Men were not ready to give up their God-given superiority. Generations of scientists accepted the theory of female inferiority and perpetuated the idea that women were overly emotional and not competent to make decisions for their own lives. Blackwell's rebuttal had little effect on the subject of equality for women, but it shined a tiny beam of light on the topic.

Eliza Burt Gamble read Darwin's work, and although she disagreed with his conclusion that women were inferior to men, she believed that evolutionary theory gave support to the women's suffrage movement. In her book *The Evolution of Woman: An Inquiry into the Dogma of Her Inferiority to Man* (1894), she surmised that Darwin was correct in concluding that humans evolved like every other living thing on earth.

However, she thought he was wrong when it came to human evolution in women. In the animal kingdom, female animals do not sit passively by, being dominated by the male. Both play equal roles for the perpetuation of their species. Her message was that women had been cheated out of the lives they deserved by the Bible, where Eve's sin placed women forever into an inferior position to men. Instead, she used Darwin's own theories to say that equality was women's biological right.

Gamble's writing shocked a conservative Christian nation but was warmly embraced by the suffragettes. Ironically, Darwin's theory contributed to feminist's considering new possibilities about

---

[95] Antoinette Blackwell, *The Sexes Throughout Nature* (G. P. Putnam's Sons, 1875).

women.[96] Rather than Eve and Adam's story ending with men ruling over women for eternity, feminists believed the Bible story could be rewritten with a new ending using evolutionary biology that showed Eve and Adam as equal apple copickers.

The first full-length study of American women's response to evolutionary theory was written by historian Kimberly Hamlin in her book *From Eve to Evolution: Darwin, Science, and Women's Rights in Gilded Age America* (2014). In it, she affirmed the role science played with the women's movement and acknowledged that it intrigued and emboldened feminists.[97] Darwin countered emerging feminism by saying, "Unchecked female militancy threatened to produce a perturbance of the races" and to "divert the orderly process of evolution."[98]

As the nineteenth century turned into the twentieth, a new model of women's role and abilities developed. The caring, private woman emerged to complement the public, rational man. This definition continued to place women at the center of the home, caring for her husband's needs, and having no voice in her greater world.

Social Darwinism and eugenics

Sir Francis Galton, Darwin's half cousin, launched a new science in Britain in 1883 that he coined *eugenics*. Borrowing from Darwin's ideas, Galton believed that the human race could be improved by ridding society of undesirables and propagating the elite. The eugenics movement was born, and supporters believed that people with undesirable traits should be prevented from having children. Undesirable people were people of color, on welfare, in mental asylums, uneducated, disabled, homeless, and of the lower classes. Naturally, the desirables were those with pedigrees and of the wealthy class.

---

[96] Jerry Bergman, "Darwin's Teaching of Women's Inferiority," Institute for Creation Research, March 3, 1994, https://www.icr.org/article/darwins-teaching-womens-inferiority/.

[97] Kimberly Hamlin, *From Eve to Evolution: Darwin, Science, and Women's Rights in Gilded Age America* (Chicago, IL: University of Chicago Press, 2014).

[98] Darwin, 168.

Social Darwinism was a set of loose ideas using Darwin's theory of survival of the fittest to suggest that some people were innately better than others and, consequently, became more powerful. Darwin saw his biological theory as a way to improve the human race through man's own manipulation and influence. He supported Francis Galton's antiwoman views, saying repeatedly that women's mental power was inferior to men's.

Darwin reinforced Galton's work in eugenics by saying,

> There is reason to believe that vaccination has pre-served thousands, who from a weak constitution would formerly have succumbed to small-pox... excepting in the case of man himself, hardly any one is so ignorant as to allow his worst animals to breed.[99]

The seeds for selective breeding through sterilization became one of the important pillars of the eugenics movement. Although the eugenics movement did not gain traction in Britain, it quickly gained widespread support in the United States, peaking in 1920 to 1930. Thirty-two states passed forced sterilization laws, resulting in sixty-four thousand Americans being sterilized. Men were steril-ized to treat their aggression and to eliminate their criminal behavior. Eugenicists predominantly targeted women to protect white racial health and weed out *defectives* in society.[100]

The Immigration Restriction League, founded in 1894 by three Harvard graduates, was the first organization associated with the eugenics movement. It specifically was formed to limit immigra-tion from what they considered inferior groups—i.e., Eastern and Southern European countries—and to prevent inferior races from polluting American genes, thus lessening the threat to a superior, civilized America. Membership of the league was comprised of all

---

[99] Ibid.

[100] "Eugenics in the United States," Lumen, https://courses.lumenlearning.com/culturalanthropology/chapter/eugenics-in-the-united-states/.

white men, including the presidents of Harvard University, Bowdoin College, and Stanford University. They wished to protect superior American genes from inferior races. One method they introduced was mandating literacy tests for immigrants, assuming that inferior people would have low literacy skills.

In 1903, the American Breeders' Association (ABA), founded by agricultural scientists, was the first US organization that had as its purpose supporting genetic and eugenic research. Membership in the ABA included Alexander Graham Bell, inventor; Charles B. Davenport, biologist; and David Starr Jordan, Stanford president (whose buildings, once named in his honor, have now been renamed). The ABA mission statement follows:

> Society must protect itself; as it claims the right to deprive the murderer of his life so it may also annihilate the hideous serpent of hopelessly vicious protoplasm. Here is where appropriate legislation will aid in eugenics and creating a healthier, saner society in the future.[101]

Eventually, the Immigration Restriction League and the American Breeders' Association joined forces for eugenic solutions to preserve the purity of America.

Ironically, well-to-do feminists had little concern about women of color and those from lower economic and social classes. Several feminist organizations supported eugenics, including the National League of Women Voters, Woman's Christian Temperance Union, and the National Federation of Women's Clubs.[102] Margaret Sanger, the leader of the birth control movement in the United States, approved of some methods of eugenics, which she incorporated into the language of her movement. Feminist women were not necessarily good friends of *all* women.

---

[101] *American Breeders Magazine* (American Breeders Association, 1910).
[102] Ransom Riggs, "The Frightening History of Eugenics in America," *Mental Floss*, February 2, 2011.

Euthanasia, or "mercy killing," was explored in this era as a method to rid defective germ plasm in the human population. The 1911 report funded by the Carnegie Institute listed eighteen ways to remove defective genetic attributes. Number 8 on the list was euthanasia.[103] In 1931, The Illinois Homeopathic Medicine Association began lobbying for "imbeciles and other defectives" to be euthanized. There was talk of setting up gas chambers, but that idea was soon abandoned. Eventually, euthanasia did not meet with Americans' approval, and other ways were designed to keep undesirables from reproducing. Instead, creative measures were employed, such as withholding treatment for babies born with defects.

The Illinois Institution for the Feebleminded in Lincoln, Illinois, was established for "feeble-minded and epileptic people." Historians speculated that institutions like this supported eugenics through backdoor methods and were "slow-acting lethal chambers." Patients at Lincoln were reportedly fed milk from cows that had been infected with tuberculous. Records stated the causes of death at these institutions as undetermined cause, exhaustion due to epileptic seizures, and tuberculous.

Medical investigators were perplexed by how the death rates could be so high at asylums like those in Lincoln, Illinois. In the 1930s, life expectancy for individuals with intellectual disabilities was about 18.5 years, and in 1990, life expectancy for individuals with intellectual disabilities was 66.2 years.[104] The wide disparity of life expectancy underscores the disdain for the lives of those who did not meet the standards of *normal* during the eugenics movement.

Adolf Hitler adopted the views of social Darwinism. Later, he found inspiration in America's eugenic policies, especially California's policy, which accounted for almost twenty thousand forced sterilizations from 1909 to 1960. Hitler hoped to build a new master race by ridding his country of those who did not have pure Aryan genes. If German women possessed the right features, they were sometimes

---

[103] Ibid.

[104] Edwin Black, "Government Death Panels and Mass Murder Were Always an Option in 20th Century America's War Against the Weak," History News Network, August 24, 2009, http://hnn.us/roundup/entries/115858.html.

bred for the fatherland. Hitler thought women should be restricted to "Kinder, Kirche, Küche" (children, church, kitchen). He modeled his master race plan, in part, on that of the United States. Hitler even sent a congratulatory letter to the Leon Whitney, president of the American Eugenics Society.[105]

One of the most famous forced sterilization cases is that of Carrie Buck. She lived with her foster parents from the age of three, after her mother was institutionalized for being classified as a low-grade idiot. Allegedly, her foster cousin raped Carrie when she was seventeen, and she became pregnant. At the request of her foster parents, Carrie was evaluated and judged to be feebleminded. Three months later, she gave birth to her child Vivian, the same month that Virginia passed a bill that allowed for state-enforced sterilization of those genetically unfit for procreation.

In June 1924, Carrie was sent to the same institution in Virginia where her mother Emma was an inmate. There, Carrie was scheduled to be sterilized by Doctor Bell. Carrie asked the courts not to allow her sterilization. On appeal, the Supreme Court heard *Buck v. Bell*, where Justice Oliver Wendell Holmes Jr. compared social undesirables to bacteria to be wiped out. He ordered Carrie to be sterilized, saying, "Three generations of imbeciles are enough."[106]

Surgeon John H. Bell performed the operation in 1927, and Carrie became the first person sterilized in Virginia. Her daughter Vivian died of an intestinal disease at age eight. Carrie later married, was widowed, and then remarried, never again able to bear children.

The story does not stop there. Carrie's sister Doris was hospitalized for appendicitis. During surgery, she was secretly sterilized. Doctors felt the obligation to rid the United States of another potential "bad apple." Doris and her husband tried for years to have chil-

---

[105] Edwin Black, "Eugenics and the Nazis—The California Connection," *San Francisco Chronicle*, November 9, 2003, https://www.sfgate.com/opinion/article/Eugenics-and-the-Nazis-the-California-2549771.php.

[106] Adam Doerr, "Three Generations of Imbeciles Are Enough," The Privacy Report, June 25, 2009, https://theprivacyreport.com/2009/06/25/three-generations-of-imbeciles-are-enough/.

dren. In the 1980s, she was devastated to learn she had unknowingly been sterilized.

Two years after the *Buck v. Bell* case allowed sterilization as permissible under the US Constitution, the Eugenics Board of North Carolina (EBNC) was formed. It passed far-reaching sterilization laws of the "mentally defective." From 1929 to 1977, the board remained in place, resulting in an estimated 7,500 people being sterilized. Of these people, five thousand are estimated to have been Black, and 85 percent of the five thousand were estimated to have been women.[107] In 1974, Virginia repealed its forced sterilization law. In 2002, Governor Mark Warner apologized for Virginia's eugenics program, and a historical marker commemorating Carrie Buck was erected in Charlottesville. North Carolina was the first state to propose paying reparations to victims of the state-sponsored sterilization program in 2014.

In 2020, Dawn Wooten, a whistleblower, filed a report that was published by the not-for-profit Project South. The report alleged that detained immigrant women received high rates of hysterectomies at the Irwin County Detention Center (ICDC) in Georgia. Interviews with immigrant women and ICDC nurses conducted by Wooten claimed that one doctor was responsible. Wooten said, "When I met all these women who had had surgeries, I thought this was like an experimental concentration camp. It was like they're experimenting with our bodies."[108] Perhaps eugenics still motivates solutions from those who have power over people considered less worthy.

---

[107] K. Begos, D. Deaver, J. Railey, and S. Sexton, *Against Their Will: North Carolina's Sterilization Program and the Campaign for Reparations* (Apalachicola, FL: Gray Oak Books, 2012).

[108] "Interview at the Irwin County Detention Center," Project South: Institute for the Elimination of Poverty and Genocide, October 2019, https://projectsouth.org/wp-content/uploads/2020/09/OIG-ICDC-Complaint-1.pdf.

Brain research

Gina Rippon writes in *The Gendered Brain* (2021),

> The so-called "female" brain has suffered centu-
> ries of being described as undersized, underde-
> veloped, evolutionarily inferior, poorly organized
> and generally defective—as being the cause of
> women's inferiority, vulnerability, emotional
> instability, scientific ineptitude, making them
> unfit for any kind of responsibility, power, or
> greatness.[109]

Almost all scientists in the 1800s believed that women
were inferior and verified their prejudices with ongoing studies.
Contemporaries of Charles Darwin conducted brain research they
believed, once and for all, would prove women were less intelligent
than men. They reasoned that women's brains were smaller and,
therefore, could not have the intellectual capacity of men's brains.

One experiment was conducted by filling male and female skulls
with birdseed. Then the birdseed was weighed. The heavier weight of
the birdseed in male skulls "proved" that women had smaller brains
than men.[110] Elaborate charts and ratings were created. These learned
men obviously did not use simple observation to conclude that wom-
en's skulls were generally smaller than men's. The false assumption
that went untested was whether brain size was related to intelligence.

Paul Broca was a well-respected scientist who was a pioneer in
attempting to prove the intellectual inferiority of women. Broca's
area, a section of the frontal lobe of the brain's dominant hemisphere,
is named for his contributions to the field of brain study. He founded
the Anthropological Society in 1859 and studied craniometry—i.e.,
facial features, jutting jaws, measurement of skulls, brain size, etc.—

---

[109] Gina Rippon, *The Gendered Brain: The New Neuroscience that Shatters the Myth
of the Female Brain* (London: Random House, 2019), xii.

[110] Stephen Gould, *The Mismeasure of Man* (New York: W. W. Norton and
Company, 1981), 83.

in order to "delineate human groups and assess their relative worth." Of all the human groups, he collected the most data comparing the brains of men with those of women.[111] Broca concluded that "the relatively small size of the female brain depends in part upon her physical inferiority and in part upon her intellectual inferiority."[112]

Gustave Le Bon, a prominent scientist, also worked to categorize women as vastly inferior to men. He strongly opposed that women in the United States were asking to have access to higher education on the same footing with men:

> A desire to give them [women] the same education, and, as a consequence, to propose the same goals for them, is a dangerous chimera... The day when women leave the home and take part in battles, on this day a social revolution will begin, and everything that maintains the sacred ties of the family will disappear.[113]

The suffrage movement was in its early stage in 1879. Women were fighting to get the vote, own land, and manage their own money, while scientists were fighting to prove them incapable. Le Bon weighted into the argument, saying,

> Women...represent the most inferior forms of human evolution and...are closer to children and savages than to an adult, civilized man. They excel in fickleness, inconsistency, absence of thought and logic, and incapacity to reason. Without a doubt there exist some distinguished women, very superior to the average man, but they are as exceptional as the birth of any monstrosity, as,

[111] Ibid., 104, 105.
[112] Ibid.
[113] G. LeBon, *Anatomical and Mathematical Researches into the Laws of the Variations of Brain Volume and their Relation to Intelligence* (1879), 60–61.

for example, of a gorilla with two heads; consequently, we may neglect them entirely.[114]

Most educated people of the time were persuasively confident
in the research. Male-female brain studies continued throughout the
twentieth century. Imaging science made the study of the brain more
sophisticated. The EEG (electroencephalogram) emerged in 1924,
and it remained the major way scientists studied brains until the
1970s.

The PET scan (positron-emission tomography system) was the
next methodology developed. It linked blood flow and brain activity. The complexity of the brain revealed that behavior results from
a combination of electrical and chemical activity. Today, even with
more modern studies and methodologies, a single theory of how the
brain works has not been reached.

Rigorous testing on boys and girls confirms that the differences
in perception of abilities between the sexes have been shaped by
biased science and by societal beliefs rather than by true superiority
of intelligence of either gender. Sadly, girls today still believe that
boys are smarter than girls.[115]

Hysteria and emotions

Hysteria was exclusively a women's mental disorder in the
nineteenth century. Today, the term is still used almost exclusively
for women. The scientific terminology for hysteria was "functional
neurological symptom disorder" (FNSD) or "conversion disorder."
Sigmund Freud coined the phrase *conversion* to describe how unre-
solved anxieties and fears can convert to psychosomatic illnesses.
FNSD is defined today as a psychiatric illness in which symptoms
cannot be explained and is predominantly diagnosed in women.

---

[114] Ibid., 62.

[115] Betty McNamara, "Girls Think Boys Are Naturally Smarter than They Are,
Study Says," *Teen Vogue*, January 26, 2017, https://www.teenvogue.com/story/
girls-think-boys-are-smarter.

The term hysteria came from the Greek word for uterus. Hippocrates described the uterus as "wandering wombs." Plato thought the uterus was a living being, and Argonato Melampus, the founder of the first medical approach to hysteria, called the uterus "an animal within an animal." All three men believed the uterus was disordered unless a penis was available for penetration. Two symptoms of uterus disorder were shortness of breath and women being sexually aggressive. Marriage and sexual intercourse were considered to be the best remedies for this illness.

In the middle ages, *possession* was added to the list of hysteria symptoms. Single and elderly women who were not sexually active, weak, and easily influenced were thought to be more susceptible to Satan and demonic forces. The label of *possession* resulted in witchcraft trials held across the world, where women were targeted, put on trial, and executed for being witches.

Hysteria became an area of medical focus in the nineteenth century with an ever-expanding list of symptoms, including inability to speak, fainting, emotionality, irrational behavior, and sexually unrestrained thinking. Suspiciously, this focus coincided with the women's suffrage movement. By 1895, physicians claimed that one-fourth of all women suffered from hysteria.[116] Feminism and hysteria were linked together during the suffrage campaign. In 1908, the *London Times* editorialized,

> One does not need to be against women's suffrage to see that some of the more violent partisans of that cause are suffering from hysteria. We use the word not with any scientific precision, but because it is the name most commonly given to a kind of enthusiasm that has degenerated into habitual nervous excitement.[117]

---

[116] I. Veith, *Hysteria: The History of a Disease* (Chicago: University of Chicago Press, 1965), 10.

[117] Sander L. Gilman, Helen King, Roy Porter, G. S. Rousseau, and Elaine Showalter, *Hysteria beyond Freud* (Berkeley: University of California Press, 1993).

Hysteria framed women's emotionality as a biological fact. Women in the nineteenth century carried smelling salts in their handbags, and fainting couches were the fashion in case ladies swooned from excessive emotion. The obvious logic followed: why should irrational, hysterical, and emotional women be trusted with the vote?

Hysteria is a word culturally reserved for women. Men who show similar behaviors—like going to football games wearing a wedge of cheese on their heads or attending basketball games with their bodies painted in their team's colors, yelling, screaming, and wildly urging a ball to go through a hoop—are called sports fans.

Scientific psychology of the late nineteenth century looked at the differences in men's and women's emotions. Once again, men did the research and found, not surprisingly, that men's emotions were noble, revealing passion, and helping men to higher levels of reason. Women's emotions were a result of hormones, resulting in lack of stability, poorly organized thinking, and emotional behavior. For men, honor rested in defending women from sexual harm, often fighting duels to protect women's honor. If a woman had been compromised by a man, the honorable man did his duty and married the disgraced women. Honor in a woman was exclusively linked to her own sexual behavior. Once a woman was dishonored, she could never recover from her fall from grace. Not so with a man. He had ample opportunities to recover his honor, reestablish his reputation, and sometimes, become a hero.

Men's cures for women's health

Since men found the disorders in women, they also found the cures. Of course, hanging or burning at the stake was a permanent cure for the "magical-demonological disorder," but additional cures for women's issues were developed.

The uterus was considered to be the nerve center in the female body from which illness was disseminated. When the uterus was displaced, illnesses such as headaches, depression, and fatigue resulted. Pelvic massage, also known as the Brandt method, was named for the Swedish doctor who developed it. Pelvic massage was performed by a doctor inserting a finger into the vagina and manipulating the womb to restore it to the right position. The practice fell out of favor around 1920, when science affirmed the source of women's pathological issues was not the uterus but rather the neurotic brain. Women's issues were then deemed psychological.[118]

Isaac Baker Brown, a fellow of the College of Surgeons in London, published *On the Curability of Certain Forms of Insanity, Epilepsy, Catalepsy, and Hysteria in Females* (1866). His cure was a clitorectomy, the surgical removal of the clitoris. In the nineteenth century, few doctors could have located the clitoris due to its lack of reference in medical textbooks. Brown claimed a clitorectomy treated a wide range of feminine problems (in addition to those listed in the book's title), including mental illness, idiocy, masturbation, a distaste for marriage, and women answering back. He claimed that after the operation, a woman "became in every respect a good wife."[119]

In the United States, FGM (female genital mutilation) was also used to treat hysteria, depression, nymphomania, and frigidity. Logic suggests that women might feel hysterical, frigid, and depressed if their clitoris had been mutilated. The federal law, Female Genital Mutilation Act, 1996, banned FGM on any woman under age sixteen. Then, in 2018, Bernard A. Friedman, Michigan federal judge, struck down the ban as unconstitutional. He also ordered that charges be dropped against eight people who had mutilated the genitals of nine girls. The Department of Justice decided not to appeal the ruling. As of August 2019, thirty-five individual states have made specific laws that prohibit FMG, while the remaining states have not acted on this issue.[120]

---

[118] Michaela Malmberg, "Gynecological Massage: Gender, Conflict, and the Transfer of Knowledge in Medicine During the Fin de Siècle," in *Explorations in Baltic Medical History, 1850–2015*, ed. Nils Hansson and Jonatan Wistrand (Rochester, NY: University of Rochester Press, 2019), 43, 48.

[119] Helen King, "The Rise and Fall of FGM in Victorian London," *The Conversation*, March 12, 2015, https://theconversation.com/the-rise-and-fall-of-fgm-in-victorian-london-38327.

[120] Robert Snell, "Genital Mutilation Ruled Unconstitutional, Judges Drops Charges against Sect," *Detroit News*, November 21, 2018.

Silas Weir Mitchell, MD, developed the "rest cure" in the 1870s to address several ailments including neurasthenia (a term no longer used today). Neurasthenia was defined as the result of exhaustion of the central nervous system's energy reserves. His patients were generally women of the upper middle-class. The rest cure spread through the United States and England with husbands giving consent and wives not being allowed to weigh in on their own health decisions. The rest cure removed all stimuli from a patient for up to eight weeks. This meant total isolation—no reading, no speaking, no writing, no anything. Some patients were not even allowed to turn over in bed without help. Very few patients found the cure helpful. Most found it intolerable, and many sunk into deep depression.

Charlotte Perkins Gilman wrote a short story, *The Yellow Wallpaper* (1892), published in *New England Magazine*. Gilman based the story on her own diagnosis as a hysteric, although with today's hindsight, she was probably suffering from postpartum depression. Her doctor, Dr. Mitchell, was unsympathetic to women diagnosed with hysteria. He prescribed the "rest cure," and Gilman's husband concurred, while Gilman herself had no say in her own treatment. In *The Yellow Wallpaper*, the hysteric woman character was assigned only one occupation: to stare at yellow wallpaper for weeks. The cure moved her from depression to insanity.

Through her writing, Gilman argued for equality in biology. She claimed there was no female mind, nor was the brain an organ different in the sexes. She said these ideas were as insensible as talking about a *female* liver.

Dr. Mitchell's career suffered as a result of Gilman's book, and the rest cure was eventually abandoned as a treatment for mental health issues. *The Yellow Wallpaper* was regarded as one of the important early feminist literary works because of its depiction of attitudes about women's physical and mental health in the nineteenth century.

Feminine beauty, femininity, and the right look for women

Stephanie Shields examined British and American psychology ideal of femininity and masculinity in the late nineteenth century.

She explained that being feminine had a strict set of cultural expectations for those in the upper classes, much of which was centered on the job of getting a husband.[121]

Jane Austen's social commentary looked at the challenges of being a woman at the end of the eighteenth century with an insightful and ironic presentation on the status of women. The daughters of gentlemen lived by rigid social conventions with complete dependence on men and a need to marry or face the choices of languishing as a poor relation in homes of their relatives, serving as a governess, or becoming a companion to an elderly lady.

In Jane Austen's novel *Pride and Prejudice*, the ideal of femininity is defined by Caroline Bingley, an aristocratic snob. She condescendingly describes the ideal woman to Elizabeth Bennet, the feisty central character. Bingley says she knows only six women who are accomplished:

> A woman must have a thorough knowledge of music, singing, drawing, dancing, and the modern languages, to deserve the word; and besides all this, she must possess a certain something in her air and manner of walking, the tone of her voice, her address and expressions...and to all this she must yet add something more substantial, the improvement of her mind by extensive reading.[122]

Elizabeth replies, "I am no longer surprised at your knowing only six accomplished women. I rather wonder at your knowing any."

In the nineteenth century, an ideal woman should not be seen as an intellectual. The thinking of the time was that women who were too intelligent were unfeminine, pretentious, and unmarriage-

---

[121] S. A. Shields, "Passionate men, emotional women: Psychology constructs gender difference in the late 19th century," *History of Psychology* 10, no. 2 (2007): 92–110.

[122] Jane Austen, *Pride and Prejudice* (Penguin Classics, 1813), 39.

able. It was required for a woman to appear less intelligent than her husband and never to best him in games, activities, or intellect.

Charles Darwin made a similar observation when discussing the differences between men and women:

> If two lists were made of the most eminent men and women in poetry, painting, sculpture, music (inclusive of both composition and performance), history, science, and philosophy, with half-a-dozen names under each subject, the two lists would not bear comparison. We may also infer that…the average of mental power in man must be above that of women.[123]

Darwin did not factor that women were barred from higher education, and societal norms kept women from wanting to appear intelligent (lest they not catch husbands). They could not manage their own money or property and were dependent on their husbands' wishes. I, like Elizabeth Bennet, am no longer surprised at there being so few women of accomplishment on Darwin's lists. I rather wonder at there being any.

Galton, of eugenics fame, was also considered the father of statistics. Numbers, statistics, and charts add credibility to scientific experiments. Galton created a "beauty map" of women in Britain. He secretly graded the beauty of British women on a scale from the most repulsive to the most attractive, complete with ratings and numbers. He tried to quantify beauty and make it scientific. Galton put Aberdeen women at rock bottom on the beauty-ugly scale.[124] We are not clear how he intended to use these data, but it might have connected with his views of perpetuating the best and most beautiful women's gene pools. On June 20, 2020, the Galton Lecture Hall

---

[123] Darwin, 361.

[124] Jim Holt, "Measure for Measure: The Strange Science of Francis Galton," *The New Yorker*, January 16, 2005, https://www.newyorker.com/magazine/2005/01/24/measure-for-measure-5.

went the way of other racists and misogynists and was renamed at the University College London (UCL).

The idea that women should conform to physical attractiveness standards is timeless and varies from culture to culture. In the United States, the concept of ideal feminine beauty has resulted in eating disorders and women suffering from depression and low self-esteem. These conditions continue through adulthood, resulting in women often being dissatisfied with who they are and how they look. The issues of self-loathing and depression with teenage girls on Instagram is an extension of the beauty quotient expectations in the decade of the 2020s.

The achievements of women like Mary Cassatt and Dr. Marie Curie are even more to be marveled at in light of the discrimination of their time. Cassatt, a famous American painter and contemporary of Darwin, became acquainted with Ingres, Degas, Corot, and Pissarro at the Paris World's Fair of 1855. Art was a socially acceptable skill for a woman in which to dabble, but it was not acceptable to become a professional artist. Cassatt studied art in the United States but was not allowed to draw from a live model. She left for Paris in 1866, where she was a painter and printmaker, and became the only American female artist to exhibit with the Impressionists. Throughout her life, she overcame barrier after barrier to produce the amazing works of art that we treasure today.

About ten years after Darwin's death in 1891, Dr. Curie studied chemistry and physics at the Sorbonne in Paris because she was not allowed to study in Poland. She eventually became the first woman to win a Nobel Prize, the first person to win two Noble Prizes, and the only person to win the prize in two different areas. Think of the uphill battles for women to take their places in their various fields of study. Imagine the contributions women could have made in every field if they had been allowed.

Angela Saini, in her book *Inferior*, concludes,

> Feminism can be a friend to science. It not only improves how science is done by pushing researchers to include the female perspective,

but science in turn can show us that we're not as different as we seem. Research to date suggests that humans survived, thrived, and spread across the globe through the efforts of everyone equally sharing the same work and responsibilities. For most of our history, we lived hand in hand. And our biology reflects this.[125]

In the first neurological study of children's math aptitude using brain scans, Dr. Jessica Canton, professor of developmental neurology at Carnegie Mellon University, says there is no math aptitude gender difference. She does suggest that the *belief* that boys are stronger in STEM subjects still persists, and that cultural norms are likely steering girls and young women away from STEM fields.[126]

Scientists have spent much time conducting research to prove women as inferior instead of celebrating ways that women add to and enhance areas of everybody's lives. Think of the opportunities and achievements that have been missed. At the end of all men's efforts to prove women inferior, multiple modern research studies, as well as our own everyday observations, have established that there is no difference in intelligence between the average man and the average woman.[127]

[125] Angela Saini, *Inferior* (Beacon Press, 2017), 180.
[126] Katie Hunt, "Brain Scans Don't Lie: The Minds of Girls and Boys Are Equal in Math," CNN, November 8, 2019, https://www.cnn.com/2019/11/08/health/math-boys-girls-brains-scn/index.html.
[127] Roberto Colom, "Negligible Sex Differences in General Intelligence," *Intelligence* 28, no. 1 (2000): 57–68, https://www.researchgate.net/.

CHAPTER 6

Our Feminist Foremothers

The feminist movement probably had its beginnings when Eve sat down and confided in her oldest daughter that she had unfairly received the blame for the expulsion from the Garden of Eden.
—Alleen Pace Nilsen,
Linguistic Sexism as a Social Issue

The history of feminism is a complicated and messy story with abundant characters and plotlines, often telling the narrative from different perspectives, including those of race and class. Throughout the feminist movement, groups have aligned, broken apart, and had differing agendas. Our understanding of who we are as women and how we have come to where we are today is helpful in understanding our ongoing journey toward equality.

How did the demand for women's right to vote begin? What were the barriers that needed to be overcome? Mary Wollstonecraft, considered one the first feminist philosophers, kicked off the concept of women's equity in England in her 1792 famous essay, *A Vindication of the Rights of Woman*. Her argument was that women were not inherently inferior to men but that they lacked education. Wollstonecraft believed that women and men should be treated equally, and social order should be based on reason. Her essay resonated with women in America, and discussions of women's equality began to force opinions on the issue.

American feminism had its roots in the abolitionist movement, and women's equality was an unpopular cause in both the North and South. Women were struggling with patriarchy, and the antislavery movement was struggling with racism. The two causes were brought together by the common goals of social reform and liberation from oppression. Men and women began working together, unusual for the times, to advance both causes.

Northern reformer William Lloyd Garrison was the editor of the antislavery paper *The Liberator*. He and Arthur Tappan created the *American Anti-Slavery Society* (AASS), with its first convention meeting in Philadelphia in December 1833. Women could not be delegates to the convention, but four women were allowed to observe, including Lucretia Mott, a Quaker who believed in the equality of all. Garrison asked delegates to sign his Declaration of Sentiments of the Anti-Slavery Society, which detailed the evils of slavery.

As the request was being debated, Lucretia Mott asked if she could speak. She stood and asked her husband, James, to sign the Declaration of Sentiments. The men at the convention were impressed with Mott and encouraged the women in attendance to start their own female antislavery group. Three days later, Mott and twenty-one other women created the interracial Philadelphia Female Anti-Slavery Society (PFASS).[128] Their work continued in the face of proslavery activists who were appalled that white women were working with men *and* Blacks. Tensions ran high when the second Anti-Slavery Convention of American Women was held five years later (1838). Enraged proslavery mobs revengefully burned Philadelphia Hall to the ground.[129]

The seeds of the feminist movement began over tea on July 13, 1848, when five ladies discussed the plight of women of the day: no voting rights, no ability to own property, no right to manage their own money, and little access to education. They decided, over cake, to organize the first women's right's convention in Seneca Falls,

---

[128] Rosalyn Terborg-Penn, *African American Women in the Struggle for the Vote, 1850–1920* (Bloomington: Indiana University Press, 1997), 13–35.

[129] Richard S. Newman, *The Transformation of American Abolitionism: Fighting Slavery in the Early Republic* (Chapel Hill, NC: UNC Press, 2002).

New York. Two of the women who were present were Lucretia Mott and Elizabeth Cady Stanton. They were frustrated for having been excluded from the World Anti-Slavery Convention in London eight years earlier, only because they were women. Mott and Stanton, along with other women, took the lessons they had learned from their work with the Anti-Slavery movement—organizing, advocating, writing, lobbying, and public speaking—and translated these experiences into the fight for women's equal rights.

The tea party ladies put a notice in the Seneca Falls newspaper, inviting all women to attend the first women's rights convention. This historic two-day meeting resulted in a commitment that began the national movement for women's rights and equality.

On the first day of the convention, Elizabeth Cady Stanton read the Declaration of Sentiments and Resolutions, which detailed a list of women's grievances. It also called for the right for women to vote. Stanton drafted and modeled the sentiments on the United States Declaration of Independence, saying, "We hold these truths to be self-evident: that all men and women are created equal; that they are endowed by their creator with certain unalienable rights."

On the second day of the convention, abolitionist and escaped slave Frederick Douglas was one of the few men invited to speak. Douglas, a longtime supporter of women's rights, gave a stirring speech aimed at unifying the causes of Blacks and women. He emphasized achieving the universal goals of equality by support for Blacks and women's voting rights. On the strength of his speech, the convention voted on the Declaration of Sentiments and Resolutions with sixty-eight women and thirty-two men signing the document that demanded the right for women to vote. The suffrage movement had begun.[130]

The sentiments did not go unnoticed. An article in the *Daily Oneida Whig* newspaper, written by an anonymous author, entitled "Bolting by Ladies," stated, "Was there ever such a dreadful revolt?

---

[130] Barbara Matusow, "The Remarkable Friendship of Susan B. Anthony and Frederick Douglass," One Woman One Vote Festival, 2020, http://2020owovfest.org/susan-b-anthony-and-frederick-douglass/.

They set aside the statute *wives submit yourself onto your husbands.*" The author calls the convention "the most shocking and unnatural incident ever recorded in the history of womanity… Where husbands, will be our dinners, our elbows, our domestic firesides and the holes in our socks?"[131] Perhaps the author wrote this article anonymously because he did not want to face the wrath of his own wife nor other women who were becoming alarmingly outspoken.

The first wave

The feminist movement has been described metaphorically as *waves* that suggests a congruence of thinking as each wave swells and recedes in gentle harmony. In actuality, the various waves overlapped and crashed into each other, with rigid opinions about who should be a part of the movement and what the agendas, strategies, and goals should be. Examining the waves of feminism is helpful in seeing the context of the times, the eras, and the issues that were and still persist as women work to advance their rights. Looking at each era's failures and accomplishments adds to the understanding of women's long journey to equality.

First wave feminism, from the late nineteenth to the early twentieth century, was also known as the suffrage movement. The right to vote was put into the US Constitution in 1787, but it was intended only for white men. Suffrage was originally a term that meant prayer. Eventually, suffrage was used by men of color to mean the unalienable right to vote. Women adopted the word *suffrage* as their own, and it has now come to be associated with securing voting rights for women.

First-wave fissures began to appear almost immediately as woman brought differing perspectives forward. Some women opposed suffrage because they believed women's traditional roles need not be changed or that suffrage went against the Bible's teachings of obedience to men. Other women felt the movement was too

---

[131] *Daily Oneida Whig*, August 1, 1848, https://senecafallscoverage.tumblr.com/post/78771482216/oneida-whig.

broad, focusing on multiple areas of equal rights, not just the women's vote. Still others felt the movement did not go far enough and wanted results at a faster pace. Finding consensus in the earliest times of the movement would be a continuing hallmark for future feminist movements

Two of the important leaders for suffrage were Elizabeth Cady Stanton and Susan B. Anthony. Together, they were a formidable team who supported each other throughout their lives, always with the goal of moving women to a place of greater equality.

Stanton, a mother of seven, was an educated woman who wrote eloquently. She believed deeply that legal reforms were necessary for improving women's lives. She also believed that marriage was an institution that held women captive in inferior roles. Nevertheless, she married Henry Stanton, himself a women's rights advocate, with the stipulation that the word *obey* not be used in their wedding vows. She was not called Mrs. Henry Stanton but wished to be known as her own person, Elizabeth Cady Stanton.

Stanton was interested in reforms for women beyond gaining the right to vote. At the time of her marriage, women were considered the possession of their husbands. All property, even the property a woman owned when she came into the marriage, was passed on to other men when a husband died. As early as 1836, women lobbied the New York State Legislature to pass the Married Women's Property Law, allowing them to retain the property they owned when they married and the property that was acquired during their marriage. Stanton joined the lobbying effort in 1843, and the law passed in 1848, shortly before the Seneca Falls convention.

This success brought attention to the fledgling women's movement. Stanton went on to champion reforms to the initial law and spoke to the New York joint session of the Judiciary Committee in 1853. She harkened to her abolitionist days, saying,

> The prejudice against color, of which we hear so much, is no stronger than that against sex. It is produced by the same cause—The negro's skin and the woman's sex are both prima facie evi-

dence that they were intended to be in subjection
to the white Saxon man.[132]

Seven years later, in 1860, the amendments to the Married
Women's Property Law were passed, which included women's rights
for child guardianship, to sue and be sued, and to control her own
finances. Stanton was an unconventional woman who balanced her
interests of a large family with a fierce advocacy for women's rights
and other repressive issues of the times.

Susan B. Anthony was Stanton's closest friend and ally. Anthony
was a tireless campaigner for the suffrage movement. She did not
marry or have children because she did not want to be detracted
from her singular purpose of attaining the vote for women. Anthony
and Stanton sometimes clashed on approach and agendas, but they
always came back together to fight another day for the rights of
women. Their clashes often came down to Anthony's advocating for
one issue: that of gaining the vote for women, while Stanton wanting reform broadly for many benefits for women. Anthony thought
that campaigning for other issues diluted the energy of the suffrage
movement. Together, they founded the American Equal Rights
Association (AERA) in 1866. Black activist women and men joined
the call for women's rights, including Harriet Tubman, Sojourner
Truth, Frederick Douglas, and Robert Purvis.

Susan B. Anthony and Frederick Douglas were close friends,
and both supported universal suffrage, the right for both Blacks and
women to attain the vote. Douglas and Anthony often were paid
speakers at the same antislavery events, and not infrequently, they
were subjected to abuse, harassment, and threats by proslavery men.

In 1868, with the introduction of the Fifteenth Amendment,
a rift sharply divided the friendships of Douglas, Stanton, and
Anthony. The Amendment proposed the vote for Black men but did
not mention women. To protest, Stanton and Cady accepted the help

---

[132] Elizabeth C. Stanton, "Address to Judiciary Committee of the New York State
Legislature," Iowa State University, January 1, 1860, https://awpc.cattcenter.
iastate.edu/2017/03/21/a-slaves-appeal-1860/.

of a known racist to promote their view that women should not be excluded. Abolitionists were angered, including Lucretia Mott, the president of American Equal Rights Association (AERA), the group Stanton and Anthony had formed. Former coalitions fell apart, and activists had to choose which cause should take precedence: the Black vote or universal suffrage. Once again, deeply passionate views hardened on both sides of the issue, causing the AERA to split into two groups in 1869.

Stanton and Anthony formed the National Woman Suffrage Association (NWSA), which opposed the passage of the Fifteenth Amendment because women were disenfranchised. Their longtime friends and colleagues Lucy Stone, Julia Ward Howe, and others formed the rival American Women's Suffrage Association (AWSA), which worked for the passage of the Fifteenth Amendment. Both organizations supported women's suffrage as the top priority but differed on the approach to achieve it.

Anthony and Stanton (NWSA), used racist language to oppose passage of the Amendment. Anthony said, "I will cut off this right arm of mine before I will ever work for or demand the ballot for the Negro and not for the woman," and "'horrible outrages' would be perpetrated on white women if Black men got the vote." Stanton called African American men "Sambos" and "incipient rapists."[133]

Interestingly, Stone and Howe's group, AWSA, was considered the more radical and elitist group. It not only advocated the vote for women but also for changes in laws like those of equal pay and divorce. The NWSA was considered the more respectable of the two groups and focused only on women's right to vote.

Black women joined both organizations, depending on their ideology. Eventually, though, Black women felt excluded from the white-centrist suffrage groups and formed their own Black suffrage organizations. These women faced a particularly hard decision about the Fifteenth Amendment because they were affected by being Black

---

[133] Brent Staples, "How the Suffrage Movement Betrayed Black Women," *The New York Times*, July 28, 2018, https://www.nytimes.com/2018/07/28/opinion/sunday/suffrage-movement-racism-black-women.html.

and being women. Which choice was best? Work for Black men to get the vote and hope it provided a foot in the door for women or insist that women be a part of the bargain? Two Black women who had differing opinions on the Fifteenth Amendment were Mary Ann Shadd Cary and Sojourner Truth.

Cary's family had been active in helping secure freedom for slaves. Congress passed the Fugitive Slave Act in 1850, which deprived fugitive slaves of all rights and inflicted severe penalties on those who aided slaves. In response, Cary went to Canada with other Black Americans. There, she became the first Black female newspaper editor in North America when she published *The Provincial Freeman*, an antislavery newspaper. She returned to the United States at the beginning of the Civil War and became involved with Lucy Stone's AWSA. She advocated for the Fifteenth Amendment at a House Judiciary Committee hearing but was also critical of it not giving women the right to vote.[134]

Sojourner Truth took a different view of the Fifteenth Amendment. She advocated for universal suffrage, believing that Black women would continue to face prejudice and discrimination until their voice was heard. Truth was an escaped slave who had been sold to a cruel slave owner at the age of nine. She was sold several more times, and she escaped when her owner reneged on a promise to free her. She later said, "I did not run off, for I thought that wicked, but I walked off, believing that would be all right."[135] Truth took one of her five children with her when she walked away. She met Frederick Douglas in 1844 and, through his influence, became an important equal rights activist. She became the first woman to sue a white man and win her case against him for selling one of her children.[136]

---

[134] "Mary Ann Shadd Cary—Activist, Teacher, & Writer," *Legends of America*, http://www.legendsofamerica.com/mary-ann-shadd-cary/.

[135] "Sojourner Truth—quotes, facts & speech," October 29, 2009, https://www.history.com/.

[136] Megan Bailey, "Suffrage in America: The 15th and 19th Amendments: Between Two Worlds: Black Women and the Fight for Voting Rights," History.com,

The friendships between Anthony, Stanton, and Frederick Douglas somehow survived through this turbulent time. Douglas remained a lifelong supporter of women's rights and eventually backed Anthony and Canton's NWSA. In his speech to the International Council of Women in 1888, he said, "We are pointed to the fact that men have not only always ruled over women, but that they do so rule everywhere, and they easily think that a thing that is done everywhere must be right."[137] After twenty-one years of operating independently, the two rival women's groups merged in 1890 and became the National American Woman Suffrage Association (NAWSA).

Britain's women's rights movement was occurring at about the same time as the United States's movement, but it was more militant. In 1907, American Quaker Alice Paul, then living in England, joined British women in campaigning for suffrage. After Paul returned to the US, she initially joined the National American Woman Suffrage Association, which focused on state-by-state campaigns. Paul was more interested in federal legislation and lobbied Congress for a constitutional amendment for the vote.

In 1913, Paul and other militants formed an organization that eventually became the National Woman's Party (NWP). Alice Paul met with President Wilson, who said he did not believe it was the right time for an amendment for the women's vote.[138] People were grappling with new ideas of women's changing roles and exploring the new definition of what women were demanding for themselves. *The New York Times* printed an article in January 1914, where William T. Sedgwick, a noted biologist, talked about the pretensions of those who supported the "new doctrine for women." He claimed

https://www.nps.gov/articles/black-women-and-the-fight-for-voting-rights.htm.

[137] Frederick Douglass, "Frederick Douglass on Woman Suffrage: A Speech Before the International Council of Women, in Washington, DC," Social Welfare History Project, April 1888, https://socialwelfare.library.vcu.edu/woman-suffrage/frederick-douglass-woman-suffrage-1888/.

[138] "Alice Paul," ed. Debra Michaels, National Women's History Museum, 2015, https://www.womenshistory.org/education-resources/biographies/alice-paul.

that if the women's movement succeeded, it would throw the world back a thousand years.[139]

One month later, with the risk of the world being thrown back a thousand years, the first feminist mass meeting was held at the People's Institute, Cooper Union, New York, New York, on February 17, 1914. The second feminist mass meeting followed three days later. The overarching theme of these two meetings was *what is feminism?*

At the first meeting, six women and six men talked about what feminism meant to them. More men were in attendance than women. At the second meeting, seven women talked about various rights that women were demanding, including the right for women to work, to have their own convictions, to have their own name, to organize; and [smile] to ignore fashion. At the end of these historic two days, feminism was defined as a worldwide revolt against all artificial barriers that laws and customs interpose between women and human freedom.[140]

With growing determination, Paul organized more than one thousand women suffragists known as "Silent Sentinels," who picketed Woodrow Wilson's White House from January 1917 to June 1919. They stood silently holding signs that read, "Mr. President, how long must women wait for liberty?" Thirty women, including Alice Paul, were arrested on the charge of obstructing traffic and sentenced to seven months in prison. Paul organized a hunger strike while in prison. She was threatened to be sent to an insane asylum and to be force-fed (as had been done when she was in prison in Britain).

Sympathy for the women grew as people followed the news stories of women's continued fight for the vote.[141] A district court

---

[139] George MacAdam, "Feminist Revolutionary Principle Is Biological Bosh," *The New York Times*, January 18, 1914, https://www.nytimes.com/1914/01/18/archives/feminist-revolutionary-principle-is-biological-bosh-prof-william-t.html.

[140] "What Is feminism?" Women and the American Story, 2021, https://wams.nyhistory.org/modernizing-america/fighting-for-social-reform/what-is-feminism/.

[141] "Alice Paul."

overturned all the jailed women's sentences in 1918. Then the same month, President Wilson, without fanfare, signed the Susan B. Anthony Amendment (drafted by her in 1878), which later became known as the Nineteenth Amendment, which granted women the right to vote.

Ida B. Wells was born into slavery in 1862 in Mississippi and was freed by the Emancipation Proclamation. In 1884, she was ejected from a Tennessee train for refusing to sit in the African American section. She became a journalist to give voice to the antilynching movement. Wells was the author of *The Red Record*, which tabulated statistics and alleged cases of lynching in the United States, and then reported her findings through her journalism.[142] She battled both racism and sexism. She personified the plight of Black women of these times.

Her efforts raised the ire of whites, and she was forced to move to Chicago in 1892. There, she married Ferdinand Barnett and began to focus on the women's suffrage movement. She was a cofounder of the National Association for the Advancement of Colored People (NAACP) in 1909 in response to the Springfield, Illinois, race riots. She established the Alpha Suffrage Club in 1913, where she encouraged Black women to become more involved in politics.

Wells-Barnett traveled with sixty other Black Illinois delegates to Washington, DC, in March, 1913, where the first suffrage parade was organized by Alice Paul, Lucy Burns, and the National American Woman Suffrage Association (NAWSA). Wells-Barnett and the other Black delegates were told to march at the back of the parade because the organizers didn't want to upset the Southern delegates. Wells-Barnett stood her ground and said, "Either I go with you or not at all," and initially, she did not join the parade. She waited on the sidelines of the parade, and as the Illinois delegation marched by, she stepped in and marched along with them, supported by several white suffragettes.[143] Today, Wells-Barnett is remembered for her antilynch-

---

[142] Ida B. Wells-Barnett, *The Red Record: Tabulated Statistics and Alleged Causes of Lynching in the United States* (The Project Gutenberg, 2005).

[143] Jane Duran, "Ida B. Wells and the Forces of Democratization," *Ethnic Studies Review* 35, no. 1. (2012), https://scholarscompass.vcu.edu/esr/vol35/iss1/9/.

ing crusade and relentless work for Black civil rights. She is honored in Chicago by a major street named for her: Ida B. Wells Drive.

The most successful legislation of the first wave was the passage of the Nineteenth Amendment, which gave women the right to vote. The amendment was ratified in 1920 by thirty-six states, fourteen years after Susan B. Anthony's death. In 1923, Alice Paul wrote the Lucretia Mott Amendment, which stated, "Men and women shall have equal rights throughout the United States and every place subject to its jurisdiction." The amendment was introduced to Congress annually for many years to no avail.

Paul rewrote the amendment in 1940, and it was renamed the Alice Paul Amendment and required equality of rights under the law regardless of sex. This amendment eventually became known as the Equal Rights Amendment (ERA), which fueled feminists of the future. Many women naively believed that by securing the vote, the work of equality was achieved. One hundred years after the passage of the right for women to vote, equality battles still need to be waged. After a long-fought battle to win the vote, women astoundingly do not always cast votes that benefit them and bring equality to their lives.

CHAPTER 7

Women Warriors

In the long run, Women's Liberation will of course free
men—but in the short run it's going to COST me a lot
of privilege, which no one gives up willingly or easily.

—Robin Morgan

The hard-fought battle for passage of the Nineteenth Amendment
should have paved an easier path for women to attain equality. In real-
ity, the battle had just begun. In light of the Nineteenth Amendment,
women recognized more issues that needed to be addressed, including women's reproductive freedom, domestic violence, limited economic opportunities, and access to education. Black women, who
won the right to vote, had difficulty casting their votes. Securing
the vote did not change societal pressure that insisted women's roles
were primarily in the home. As the first wave of feminist thought
culminated, the women's movement began to fade and splinter. The
women who had been the architects of the suffrage movement could
not forge agreement on the best way forward. New women warriors
came to the rescue.

A young woman named Gloria Steinem wrote an article for
Esquire magazine in 1962. In it, she opined that women were forced
to choose between marriage and a career, unlike men. One year later,
Betty Friedan published *The Feminine Mystique*, which challenged
traditional thinking that women could find fulfillment only through

marriage and children. She called systemic sexism "the problem that has no name." Friedan was convinced that women were victims of their own belief systems when they defined themselves through their husbands and children. The book sold over three million copies in three years and was read and talked about by housewives all over America. Mainstream women began making conscious decisions about marriage and children, and careers were given serious consideration. The second wave of feminism took shape.

The second wave

Friedan was considered the mother of the women's liberation movement, and Gloria Steinem was its most famous spokesperson. Friedan's *New York Times* obituary read that she "ignited the contemporary women's movement in 1963 and as a result permanently transformed the social fabric of the United States and countries around the world… [Her book] is widely regarded as one of the most influential nonfiction books of the 20th century."[144]

Women began to find alignment in their vision, influenced by prominent feminist thinkers of this time. The "second wave" focused on a broad agenda of women's personal issues, including marital rape, domestic violence, violence against women, family, discrimination, reproductive rights, workplace equality, and both legal and de facto inequalities. Feminist thinkers made a distinction between sex (the biology that makes us man or woman) and gender (how culture and society define masculine and feminine). Feminists believed that gender could be redefined. Women realized they wanted more than political equality and legislation. They wanted social equality.

The term "second wave feminism" was coined by journalist Martha Lear in *The New York Times* magazine in 1968 in the article "The Second Feminist Wave: What Do Women Want?" The second wave, also called the women's liberation movement, took place from

---

[144] "Obituary: Betty Friedan, 85; writer led U.S. feminist movement," *The New York Times*, February 5, 2006, https://www.nytimes.com/2006/02/05/world/americas/05iht-obits.html.

the early 1960s to 1980. Friedan's words, "The Personal is Political," became the most important slogan of the movement. It asked women to understand that inequalities came about because of cultural and political power structures that men created and dominated. The answer to women's personal issues called for political action.

Time magazine traditionally named a "Man of the Year." In 1976, it created a new category: "Woman of the Year." Critic Elizabeth Janeway enthusiastically described this decision: "The sky above us lifts, light pours in, no maps exist for *Time's* enlarged world. We must make them explore." *Time* stated the reason for creating this new category:

> They have arrived like a new immigrant wave in male America. They may be cops, judges, military officers, telephone linemen, cab drivers, pipefitters, editors, business executives—or mothers and housewives, but not quite the same subordinate creatures they were before. Across the broad range of American life, from suburban tract houses to state legislatures, from church pulpits to Army barracks, women's lives are profoundly changing, and with them, the traditional relationships between the sexes. Few women are unaffected, few are thinking as they did ten years—or even a couple of years—ago. America has not entirely repealed the Code of Hammurabi (woman as male property), but enough U.S. women have so deliberately taken possession of their lives that the event is spiritually equivalent to the discovery of a new continent.[145]

Second wave feminists believed that universal sisterhood was their goal. Like earlier times, the movement was largely comprised of idealistic white women who were not quick to embrace women of

---

[145] "Women of the Year: Great Changes, New Chances, Tough Choices," *Time*, January 5, 1976.

color or those from lower economic classes. Once again, the movement experienced setbacks due to the narrow views of women's needs and a lack of unity in thinking.

Black women grappled with the double challenge of being Black and being a woman. Shirley Chisholm, a bold, outspoken Black woman, ran as the first woman presidential candidate of the Democratic party in 1972. She said, "Of my two handicaps, being female puts many more obstacles in my path than being black."[146] Chisholm participated in the largely white mainstream women's liberation movement, although she was also endorsed for the presidency by the Black Panthers Party.

Other Black women took a different path. The National Black Feminist Organization (NBFO) formed in 1973 with their statement of purpose: "to address ourselves to the particular and specific needs of the larger, but almost cast-aside half of the black race in America, the black woman."[147]

In *The Trouble Between Us*, Winifred Breines details why a racially integrated women's liberation group did not develop in the United States during this time. Breines believed that although white feminists claimed to be passionately antiracist, they often held unconscious biases and were unable to see beyond their own experiences. The topics that interested Black women were segregation, the Black Power movement, struggles with class and poverty, and educational opportunities for their children.[148] The different experiences divided white and Black women and led to separate concepts of feminism.

Black women created a broad concept termed *womanism*, while white women continued with the concept of *feminism*. Unlike feminism, which focused on the issues facing middle-class white women, womanism expanded the definition of feminism to include race and class.

---

[146] Ronald E. Kisner, "Shirley Chisholm Kicks Off Campaign for U.S. Presidency," *Jet* 41, no. 20 (February 1972): 12.

[147] Wada Kayomi, National Black Feminist Organization, 1973–1976, www.blackpast.org.

[148] 6. Winifred Breines, *The Trouble Between Us: An Uneasy History of White and Black Women in the Feminist Movement* (Oxford University Press, 2006).

Radical feminism

While not considered a separate wave, radical feminism developed within the women's liberation movement in the 1960s. Many people in the United States already thought of feminists as extreme. Few were ready for the radical feminists who embraced an even more militant stance than their moderate sisters. They wanted to speed up the molasses-slow creep toward women's equality and address issues that formerly were not spoken about.

Radical feminism was formed by women who had been active in the Vietnam antiwar effort and the New Left political movement. These activist women had campaigned for a broad range of issues from drug policy reform to feminism and civil rights. They expected to be included and empowered side by side with men in addressing the next important societal challenges, but they found themselves sidelined much as before. One stunning example was when the New York State Joint Legislative Committee on Public Health held hearings on abortion reform in 1969. The list of expert speakers included fourteen men and one Catholic nun.

The response by women was the formation of a radical feminist group, Redstockings. The group's name was a reference to Bluestockings, the derogatory label used to describe educated women in earlier centuries. The Redstockings held their own hearing, where they asked their experts, twelve women who had had abortions, to share their experiences. Gloria Steinem, who herself had an abortion at age twenty-two, attended the meeting and considered it a turning point for her as a feminist activist.[149] Incidentally, Redstockings today is a grassroots activist think tank that educates and advances the women's liberation agenda.[150]

Radical feminists believed that patriarchy had oppressed and dominated women from the beginning of time and throughout

---

[149] Edith Evans, "Women Break Up Abortion Hearing: Shouts for Repeal of Law Force Panel to Move," *The New York Times*, February 14, 1969, https://www.nytimes.com/1969/02/14/archives/women-break-up-abortion-hearing-shouts-for-repeal-of-law-force.html.

[150] Redstockings.org.

world cultures. Consequently, they turned their focus on ending male supremacy by radically reordering government, organizations, and structures built and maintained by men. They were skeptical of political action and organizations that claimed to stand for women's liberation but were administered by men. Radical feminists asserted that men were defined as "the norm" and women defined as "the other," and they worked to neutralize traditional gender roles on sexuality.

Andrea Dworkin, a radical feminist leader, brought new insights to women about rape, prostitution, and pornography by linking these issues to violence against women. Shulamith Firestone, a radical feminist writer and thinker, wrote one of the classic books on feminist thought when she was just twenty-five years old. She said,

> The end goal of feminist revolution must be, unlike that of the first feminist movement, not just the elimination of male privilege, but of the sex distinction itself. Genital differences between human beings would not matter culturally.[151]

Radical feminists did not agree on homosexuality, transgender identity, or even on heterosexual sex. Some advocated celibacy or lesbianism as an alternative to sexual relations between men and women. Those who opposed transgender people became known as TERFs (trans-exclusionary radical feminists). TERFs had strange bedfellows when they partnered with conservatives to try to ban medical support treatment for trans youth. Radical feminism became an easy target for ridicule from the opposition. Ethnic viewpoints also divided the movement. White women saw gender as the most pervasive reason for discrimination. For them, issues of gender took precedence over Black women's concerns about race and poverty.

The Equal Rights Amendment (ERA), proposed earlier by Alice Paul and the National Woman's Party, became the focal point

---

[151] Shulamith Firestone, *The Dialectic of Sex: The Case for Feminist Revolution* (William Monroe and Company, 1970).

of the women's liberation movement, and it became associated with the radical feminist's militant end of the spectrum. The ERA called for an end to discrimination by gender, including equal pay for equal work, access to credit, and increased educational and professional opportunities. One issue that complicated the passage of the ERA was that some radical feminists wanted lesbian and abortion rights as issues for inclusion, while others did not. The divisions within the second wave over these and other issues caused moderates and liberal feminists, once again, to disagree on clear messaging of ERA.

Second wave feminism, with its radical wing, scared people. Radical feminists influenced the women's liberation movement by being the first to talk about sexual politics that included sexual harassment, reproductive freedom, marital rape, domestic violence, abortion, and the role of lesbians in the movement. Feminism was painted with a broad brush. Critics portrayed these women as combative, men-hating, angry, and in addition, having hairy armpits.

Backlash against feminism was widespread. Susan Bolotin interviewed a young woman for *The New York Times* magazine in 1982 who summarized the feelings of many women who did not want to be called feminists: "I don't think of myself as a feminist, not for me, but for the guy next door that would mean that I'm a lesbian and I hate men."[152] By the end of the second wave, white feminists began to better understand the need to include race and class as a part of the feminist agenda. Black and white feminists found some common purposes on some cross-racial political projects.

Radical feminism is credited with moving the focus of feminism beyond economic issues to those of personal issues, like reproductive freedom and sexual violence. They also can be credited with casting feminism in an increasingly harsh and negative light.

Achievements in this era were the Equal Pay Act of 1963 (which has not yet met its promised goals) and the right to apply for a mortgage. *Roe v. Wade* was the single most important legislation of the second-wave era. This landmark decision, issued in 1973 by the United

---

[152] Susan Bolotin, "The Post-Feminist Generation," *The New York Times*, November 21, 1982.

States Supreme Court, stated that a woman had a right to privacy that extended to a woman's right to have an abortion. Additionally, the court said this right must be balanced against the state's interests in regulating abortions such as protecting women's health and protecting the potential of life.[153]

A continuing national debate followed the passage of *Roe v. Wade*, along with lawsuits that divided the country into prolife and prochoice factions. This debate centers around issues such as how long into pregnancy an abortion should be granted; who has the right to choose; when is a fetus considered viable; under what circumstances an abortion should be allowed, including saving the mother's life or in the case of incest or rape. Sharp tensions still divide us today, with discussions based on religious ideology that translate into identity politics. The Supreme Court will ultimately decide if *Roe v. Wade* remains the law in the United States.

With all these complications, perhaps the greatest achievement of the second wave was that society began to change the ways in which women were viewed and how women viewed themselves. Feminists gained a better understanding that the fight for equality needed to be intersectional. The activists realized the movement could not exclude people based on gender, race, socioeconomic level, ability, or sexual orientation. They recognized how multiple oppressions layer to increase the challenges for any one person or group exponentially. Once contemplated, new thought about women could not be put back in the bottle. Despite their differences, the powerful warrior women of the second wave significantly impacted women's rights in ways that have not been equaled.

---

[153] *Roe v. Wade* 410 US 113 (19).

CHAPTER 8

Rowing through Waves

I would rather be obnoxious than complicit in my own
dehumanization… I just wanted to make sure other
girls found out about feminism. It didn't have to be
our mums' feminism; we needed to build on what they
had created and change it and make it better.

—Kathleen Hanns

Women rowed through rough waters and against strong headwinds
as they steadily kept their eyes on the destination of equality. What
started out as a straightforward objective of securing the right for
women to vote evolved into today's worldwide movement of women
intent on being equal. The feminist movement, over time, has been
a compilation of blended goals, opposing opinions, sex wars, and
just plain fighting. Feminists are not a monolith, which results in a
complex and often confusing history. Feminist groups have formed,
splintered, and reformed based on theory, values, and objectives.
General to all types of feminism, regardless of label, is the relation-
ship between men, women, and power.

Note the momentum and diversity as the feminist movement
grew:

- Liberal feminism worked within existing structures to gain
  rights for women but did not challenge the system itself.

115

The suffrage movement of the late nineteenth / early twentieth centuries is an example. It tackled legislative change as the major way that voting rights were gained.

- Radical feminism emerged within the larger women's liberation movement during the 1960s civil rights and peace protest era. These feminists argued that patriarchy and male superiority were the cause of women's oppression. They worked to overhaul and eliminate systems that contributed to gender social and economic bias. Theories of radical feminism have spread worldwide as people try to understand the oppression of people in their own countries. Radical feminism has become the stereotype of feminism.

- Cultural feminism grew out of radical feminism in the 1970s and mirrors radical feminism's focus on the differences between men and women. Unlike radical feminism, cultural feminists did not believe that existing systems needed to be eliminated and then rebuilt. Instead, this perspective promoted a theory that women have greater skills at cooperation, care, building relationships, and maintaining peace. It promoted the idea of women's superiority and assumed that if women were in more leadership roles, the world would be a kinder, more peaceful place. Feminists challenged counterproductive masculine behaviors that did not include and value women's gifts to society.

- Ecofeminism began in 1974 and promoted the ways in which nature and women could be respected in a male-centered society by reevaluating existing structures. This view embraces intuition, collaboration, and holistic connections and sees humans and the environment as a whole and not subordinate to the other. They proposed that the irony of men's long use of women's *nature* to justify discrimination should be reversed and turned into a powerful affirmation of the unique abilities that women bring to humankind.

- Marxist and Socialist feminism are closely aligned. They theorized that women were oppressed because of the economic, capitalist, and class systems. The roots of this thinking were found in Marxist writings (midnineteenth century). Marxist feminism saw that women's work as homemakers and mothers was unpaid and undervalued. They believed women needed to be compensated for their labor. Simone de Beauvoir, author of the feminist Bible *The Second Sex*, 1970, drew on Marxist beliefs and agreed that lack of economic opportunities and the class system stood in the way of the liberation of women.

- Black feminism was grounded in the belief that race, gender, class, and other individual characteristics intersect to create discrimination for individuals and groups. Kimberlé Crenshaw, professor at UCLA School of Law and Columbia Law School, coined the word *intersectionality* in 1991, saying that being Black and being a woman could not be understood independently but must be taken as interdependent interactions.[154] She is also a leading scholar in critical race theory.

Against the backdrop of a variety of diverse feminist groups and thinking, this chapter continues with the wave metaphor even though some critics no longer feel the wave description is relevant going forward. Still, the four waves of feminism offer a broad understanding of its evolution and are summarized here, each wave more complicated than the last.

Brief review of first and second waves

The first wave of feminism was the suffrage movement in the late nineteenth and early twentieth centuries. It evolved from the abolitionist and temperance movements and focused on and succeeded in granting women the right to vote. Several proper ladies gathered for tea and discussed the issues facing women, including

---

[154] Kimberle Crenshaw, "Mapping the Margins: Intersectionality, Identity Politics, and Violence against Women of Color," *Stanford Law Review* 43, no. 6 (July 1991): 1241–1299, https://www.jstor.org/stable/1229039.

inability to own property, limited access to higher education, for-bidden to manage their own money, and prohibited from voting. The early movement came from small beginnings but changed the country in big ways forever. The first wave was fraught with tensions over the Fifteenth Amendment with Black men and women fighting for the same goal of securing the vote. The amendment gave Black men the right to vote but not women. People chose which side of the ideological question they were on: securing the vote for Blacks first or organizing for universal voting rights.

The suffrage work challenged the notion that women were only meant for the domestic sphere and confronted long men-held views of fairness. The first wave ended with women winning the right to vote and focused new attention on other areas of inequality that needed to be addressed, especially women's inclusion in political decisions.

The second wave of feminism occurred between the 1960s and the 1990s. This is probably the most commonly identified period of feminism, associated with the women's liberation movement and radical feminists. It was the easiest target for antifeminists to criti-cize—women making bold headlines and generating opinions about views of sexuality, equal pay, reproductive rights, and the ERA (Equal Rights Amendment).

My women's liberation aha came about in 1964 when I stood in high heels and a bathing suit with twelve other women, being judged on a beauty scale that someone somewhere created. As we made quarter turns, allowing the judges to see our assets from every vantage, I felt something was off but could not put my finger on the problem. I, like many others in the early 1960s, had vague notions of gender fairness but couldn't actually identify what was wrong.

One of the first events of the second wave were protests against the Miss America pageant in 1968. As I and others watched, femi-nists called out social injustice and helped women develop a growing self-awareness of our place and roles in society. Watching the trail-blazers of this era define the assumptions we and others held about women, I understood that competing in bathing suit contests was not the way in which I wanted to contribute to society. Incidentally, the Redstockings (a radical feminist group whose name played on the Bluestockings from the nineteenth century) held a mock contest where a sheep was crowned Miss America.

During the second wave, the antiwar and civil rights movements as well as the rise of the New Left provided context for the mood of our country. A general feeling swept the country that women were not treated equitably. Radical feminists forged new theories, often pitting men against women as its foundation. They also became a lightning rod for antifeminists and eventually lost support among moderates. They began looking for political solutions to economic and cultural sources of injustice, using Betty Friedan's coined phrases "the personal is political" and "identity politics." Both are still used today.

The difference between sex (biological) and gender (social) began to be understood. The realization of this era was that race, class, and oppression of women were interrelated. The largest women's organization in the United States, NOW (National Organization for Women) was established in 1966 and today has five hundred thousand members. It continues to challenge all aspects of sex and gender discrimination. While the Equal Rights Amendment, which guaranteed equality between the sexes, was the big battle the second wave lost, *Roe v. Wade*, allowing women the right to abortions, was their crowning victory.

The third wave

"Confusion surrounding what constitutes third-wave feminism is in some respects its defining feature," wrote Elizabeth Evans, feminist author in 2015.[155] The goals of the third wave were more ambiguous than those of the first and second waves. The third wave was informed by postmodernism—a movement in philosophy, visual arts, architecture, literature, music, and criticism that rejected mod-

---

[155] Elizabeth Evans, *The Politics of Third Wave Feminisms: Neoliberalism, Intersectionality, and the State in Britain and the US* (London: Palgrave Macmillan, 2015), 49.

ernism—the idea that there was one correct way to create, to solve problems, or to think. In architecture, the rigid, uniform, rule-bound style of modernism was replaced by incorporating cultural reflection, ornamentation, and historical design elements. Postmodern artist Roy Lichtenstein turned comic strips into an art form. John Cage, composer, created one of the most controversial pieces of music, *4'33"*, which consists of four minutes and thirty-three seconds of silence, or as he called it, the absence of intended sounds. Postfeminists had contradictory views of the lessons from the confusing broad scope of postmodernism. Some said that feminism was no longer relevant, and others said that feminism was evolving to its next iteration.

Gloria Steinem's *Ms.* magazine published a 1992 article by Rebecca Walker, "Becoming the Third Wave." Walker watched the cringe-worthy treatment of Anita Hill when she accused Clarence Thomas of sexual harassment. Hill was verbally abused and attacked as she faced an all-white male Senate committee hearing regarding Thomas's nomination to the Supreme Court. After reflection, Walker said, "I am not a postfeminist. I am the third wave."[156] Walker added that the fight for women's equality was far from over. Hill's experience led to a new focus on areas such as pay equality and sexual harassment in the workplace.

The year after Hill's testimony was ignored by the Senate's sub-committee and Clarence Thomas was named a Supreme Court justice, three women won seats in the Senate, and twenty-four women won seats in the house of representatives. Women's issues grabbed national attention and fostered national change.

Third-wave women grew up with feminism. They were critical of the flaws that burdened the prior movements and took for granted the accomplishments made by earlier feminists. They pushed back on ideas of rigid gender roles and rules of engagement that no long applied in a postfeminist world. They believed the second wave emphasized the notion that women were victims. With new understanding, they thought the second wave initiatives were too focused on upper-middle-class white women and that it did not embrace the

---

[156] Rebecca Walker, "Becoming the Third Wave," *Ms.*, 1992, 39.

full, diverse sisterhood of America. Their conclusion: there was no right way to be a feminist. As a result, an outreach for inclusivity of all women occurred, including education about trans people and bringing trans females into the mainstream.

Generation X, people born between 1961 and '81, fueled the third wave. They were grounded in the civil-rights advancements of the second wave. They continued to advocate for issues that related to women's equality, such as marginalization of minorities, reproductive rights, and economic opportunities, while they emphasized the need for a more inclusive and nonjudgmental approach to achieving gender equality.

Third-wave feminists wanted all women to be included in the conversation and to turn it from women being victims of sexual harassment to women standing strong against perpetrators of sexual harassment. Rather than gender being considered the sole reason for disadvantage, a new understanding of intersectionality emerged that stressed how multiple issues work in combination to create discrimination.

The third wave established the link between popular culture and femininity. Romantic novels, sometimes called "chick lit," were a genre that brought condemnation from traditional feminists. They had problems seeing traditional gender roles of women finding husbands and young girls being marketed as sexy being presented in media and books. Postfeminists praised chick lit for showing strong, witty girls who navigated complicated waters and found their own definitions of what made them happy. This genre stressed that there were no rules or absolute definition of the right way to be a woman. Musicians and groups like Madonna, Bikini Kill, and Spice Girls were proof that girls controlled their own brand and brought the combination of sex appeal and strength to the stage.

A powerful impact of this era was the emerging punk music groups that hit the music scene in the early 1990s. Riot grrrl was an underground feminist punk movement that combined punk music, feminism, and politics. Punk bands provided a platform for women to address issues that affected girls and women, including rape, domestic abuse, and sexuality. Bikini Kill lead singer Kathleen

Hanna wrote the Riot Grrrl Manifesto in 1991. She ended the manifesto saying,

> BECAUSE we are angry at a society that tells us Girl=Dumb. Girl=Bad. Girl=Weak.
>
> BECAUSE we are unwilling to let our real and valid anger be diffused and/or turned against us via the internalization of sexism as witnessed in girl/girl jealousism and self-defeating girltype behaviors.
>
> BECAUSE I believe with my wholeheart-mindbody that girls constitute a revolutionary soul force that can, and will change the world for real.[157]

Embracing the word *girl*, and even making it sound tough, they argued that *girliness* was not inherently less valuable than manliness and that the rejection of it was misogynistic. Riot grrrl wanted to embrace behaviors and language that second-wave feminists had worked to reject. They wore high heels and lipstick to please themselves, not to please men. Their perspectives were integrated into the next view of feminism, which would eventually challenge the notion that women had established equal norms in the entertainment business as writers, producers, and directors.

Women began to appear online and use social media in the early 2000s to share new feminist theories, broaden their goals globally, and reach new groups of people dedicated to their causes. This wave also included feminists who pushed their agendas through creative and literary means. Lena Dunham, Beyoncé, and Lindy West are examples of directors, musicians, and writers who connected their message with a wide audience.

Bitch, founded by three women in 1996, was a magazine that wanted to talk about current issues through a feminist lens. They

---

[157] *Bikini Kill*, https://www.historyisaweapon.com/defcon1/riotgrrrlmanifesto.html.

reclaimed the word *bitch* and emphasized that women could make their own rules about being women. They did not need to be bra burners or angry. Their website stated, "Bitch Media is a mission-driven outlet committed to publishing incisive, witty, smart-as-hell feminist perspective on pop culture, media, and politics that center marginalized communities." They posed questions such as, "How do I identify?" and "Who gets to decide?" They grew from an initial startup of 300 copies of a hand stapled zine to a readership of 60 million people worldwide when they closed their doors in 2022.[158]

Women planted their high heels firmly in men-only doors. Geraldine Ferraro ran on the Democratic ticket for vice president in 1990, although reporters questioned whether a woman would be tough enough for the job. Five women were elected to the US Senate in 1993. Hillary Clinton, the third female Secretary of State, gave her famous "women's rights are human rights" speech at the UN in 1995. Ruth Bader Ginsburg became the second woman named to the Supreme Court in 1993.

Third-wave women were less united around specific goals but wanted to connect gender issues with broader social concerns. They continued working on legislation that was an extension of the second wave but also brought new energy to the rights of trans people and to protecting reproductive rights. Sex wars erupted between women who believed pornography encouraged violence against women and those who thought free choice should not prohibit it. Sex wars also included opinions about prostitution from those who believed it enslaved women and should be illegal to those who thought sex workers needed legalization and support. Women's issues were highlighted in pop culture, connecting young people to issues of violence against women, rape, and sexuality. Words like *slut* and *bitch* were embraced by women as a way of liberating themselves from men-shaming dialogue.

Major legislation of this era: the Family Medical Leave Act went into effect in 1993 to help new mothers and caregivers take time off for childbirth and illness; the Violence Against Women Act, 1994,

---

[158] BitchMedia.org

provided funds for victims of rape and domestic violence among other services; and Title IX guidelines, 1997, defined sexual harassment. Other family-friendly advancements included on-site childcare in many workplaces, flexible schedules, breastfeeding spaces, and maternity leave considerations. The third wave lacked the powerful warrior women of the first and second wave but began an inclusive culture where women could find their own identities and define who they wanted to be.

The fourth wave

The fourth wave of feminism began around 2012 in the United States and is still evolving. It is defined by intersectionality, the understanding that multiple social identities overlap to create interdependent systems of discrimination. This decade has focused primarily on violence against women, rape culture, sexual harassment, and body shaming. Like the movements before, there are differing agendas, high emotions, and various calls to action.

Fourth wave feminism has changed our national dialogue. We are in a period of defining limits, language, and boundaries for professional relationships; clarifying our collective equity goals; and understanding that women need to be in leadership roles to create systemic change. The momentum for addressing workplace issues of gender equality is building, and the power of women is emerging as one of the most forceful waves to wash over our country, with women dramatically standing on the high ground of equality and respect.

A number of groups formed in response to years of women being denied equity, each with differing approaches that focuses on a wide range of issues, including violence against women, social and racial justice, equal pay for equal work, immigration reform, affordable childcare, protecting women's reproductive rights, calling out harassment and abusers of power, and greater representation of excluded groups in politics and business. These groups assert that society will be more equitable when policies and practices incorporate the perspectives of all citizens. The word *feminism* is rarely used in the groups that have formed to address the issues of today, although the goals remain to bring equal power to women.

The 2010–2020 decade generated and reenergized a remarkable number of activist women's organizations, including Pantsuit Nation, NARAL Pro-Choice America, Planned Parenthood, National Organization for Women, Feminist Majority Foundation, Supermajority, Time's Up, and the powerful game changer, #MeToo.

Time magazine's 2017 Person of the Year honored a group of women rather than a specific person. They were called The Silence Breakers. These brave women came forward, broke the silence, and started the dialog about women's issues in the workplace. This open dialog was a "shot heard 'round the world." It fueled today's women's revolution not unlike the other "shot heard 'round the world" of the American Revolution. Both revolutions were about balance, power, and freedom.

Libby Chamberlain created Pantsuit Nation on a private Facebook and Twitter hashtag in October 2016. The pantsuit symbol stood for Hilary Clinton's 2016 presidential campaign. Members focused on immigration reform, racial justice, religious freedom, and women's reproductive rights—does the list sound familiar? At the time of the 2016 election, the group had 2.9 million members. In 2019, the group had nearly four million members.[159]

The political action group Supermajority recognizes that the power of different generations, religions, classes, ethnicities, and belief systems of women has not been harnessed. Supermajority wants to unite all women across individual lines that divide them and focus on clear strategies to move promising agendas forward. Three women joined forces to create Supermajority: Cecile Richards, former head of Planned Parenthood, a powerhouse focused on women's sexual and reproductive rights; Alicia Garza, cofounder of Black Lives Matter and a leading voice for racial justice; and Ai-jen Poo, executive director of the National Domestic Workers Alliance, which

---

[159] Danielle Kurtzleben, "'Pantsuit Nation' Serves Up Nostalgia, Uplift, Heartbreak. But Why?" NPR.org, May 9, 2017, https://www.npr.org/2017/05/09/527422101/pantsuit-nation-serves-up-nostalgia-uplift-heartbreak-but why.

advocates for women in the working class to gain benefits and political power.

Supermajority, a multiracial and intergenerational group, focuses on women's rights and with the stated goal: "building a multiracial, intergenerational movement for women's equity."[160] Their immediate organizational goal is to train and mobilize two million women to become organizers and political leaders in their communities. They hope to increase women's membership in Congress to a number that more closely reflects the 54 percent of voters who are women. Their plan consists of educating women about candidates' positions on pay equity, affordable childcare, rising maternal mortality, family leave, and a government that continues to fail women. They want to push politicians to adopt agendas that Richards calls a "women's new deal" for the twenty-first century women. Julie Pace says this effort comes at moment when women have emerged as perhaps the most powerful force in politics.[161] In October of 2019, Pantsuit Nation merged with Supermajority, bringing the substantial influence of each group together.

Perhaps the best known and most impactful movement is #MeToo, founded in 2006 by Tarana Burke. She began using the hashtag #MeToo to bring attention to sexual violence in our country. The phrase went viral in October 2017 when American actress Alyssa Milano asked other victims of sexual abuse and harassment to use the hashtag #MeToo. The tweets showed sympathy to the eighty plus women who accused Harvey Weinstein, a film producer and now convicted felon of rape, assault, and other forms of nonconsensual sex. Women remembered their own personal experiences of harassment and wanted Weinstein's victims to know that they were not alone. This movement changed all genders' perceptions of what is fun and funny and has better defined limits and boundaries for the workplace. Tarana Burke also founded the nonprofit Just BE Inc.,

---

[160] Supermajority.com

[161] Julie Pace, "New Group Launches to Harness Political Power of Women," AP News, April 29, 2019, https://apnews.com/article/ff5c22f068714e4 b9b90205089839870.

an organization that supports young girls of color who have been victims of sexual abuse.

The #MeToo movement quickly spread worldwide to South Korea, Germany, Kenya, Japan, France, China, and other countries, where women began to share and call out their experiences with sexual assault and harassment. In the United States, organizations began their own #MeToo movements. The #MeTooMilitary arose after the Department of Defense Pentagon reported that fifteen thousand sexual assaults occurred in 2016.[162] #ChurchToo formed to highlight the sexual abuse that has been widely reported in religious institutions. Universities, the Screen Actors Guild, the Olympics, among other organizations, formed their own #MeToo movements to spotlight toxic environments and widespread sexual assault and harassment prevalent in our society.

Time's Up has a similar vision to #MeToo. It was formed in 2017 to turn the energy women brought to the #MeToo movement into solutions and action. Over three hundred Hollywood women, including Reese Witherspoon, Shonda Rhimes, and Natalie Portman came together to start Time's Up. This group represents all levels of the entertainment industry grapples with the disproportionate white men dominant in their business. The Time's Up Legal Defense Fund, founded in January 2018, represents women across all lines of race, religion, and background. This has been one of the most successful GoFundMe ever. They have raised over twenty-two million dollars and have engaged more than eight hundred volunteer lawyers. Their website, TimesUpNow.com, reads, "The clock has run out on sexual assault, harassment and inequality in the workplace. It's time to do something about it."

Time's Up called out New York governor Andrew Cuomo to resign immediately in an August 3, 2021, press release, saying, "The findings of the investigation further cement the fact that the powerful can no longer hide behind their influence and threats when

---

[162] Terri Moon Cronk, "DoD Releases Latest Military Sexual Assault Report," US Department of Defense, May 1 2017, https://www.defense.gov/News/News-Stories/Article/Article/1168765/dod-releases-latest-military-sexual-assault-report/.

people they've harmed are demanding accountability and justice." This public call exposed ties between Governor Cuomo and Time's Up. Tina Tchen, the group's leader, quit after it became known that she advised the Cuomo administration after he was accused of misconduct. Times Up has committed to a complete rebuilding of the organization for the future.[163]

Women face unique challenges when seeking executive office, according to research by the Barbara Lee Family Foundation, which specializes in helping elect women to executive office. Women's strengths of collaboration, compromise, and civility help them win down ballot races where group decision-making is key. But women face a competency test about their executive decision-making that men do not. Both men *and* women question if women can be commander in chief of the highest office. Perhaps this is why women make up only 21 percent of the nation's mayors, 18 percent of governors, and 5 percent of Fortune 500 chief executives.[164] For women, American culture upholds a thin line between proving oneself capable and being seen as overly aggressive and unlikable.

The feminist movement grew in our country from a few ladies attending a tea party in 1848 to a movement that now includes millions of women worldwide who have collectively organized with their eyes on the goal of equality. The journey has been arduous, frustrating, and remarkable.

Daily reminders illustrate that many issues still need to be tackled. In some instances, we are dragged backward by riptides and must regain our balance before resuming our progress through the waves. Strength and endurance must remain constant as we continue pulling the oars through rough water for the goal of equality for all.

---

[163] "Turmoil Was Brewing at Time's Up Long Before Cuomo," *The New York Times*, August 8, 2021, https://www.nytimes.com/2021/08/21/us/times-up-metoo-sexual-harassment.html.

[164] Jay Newton-Small, "Female Presidential Candidates Have to Overcome Sexism—of Other Women," *The Washington Post*, May 19, 2019, https://www.washingtonpost.com/outlook/female-presidential-candidates-have-to-overcome-the-sexism-of-other-women/2019/05/17/fc72b9ba-7755-11e9-b7ae-390de4259661_story.html.

CHAPTER 9

Anti-Feminism

It would be a much better country if women did not vote. That is simply a fact. In fact, in every presidential election since 1950, except for Goldwater in '64—the Republican would have won, if only the men had voted.

—Ann Coulter

Elizabeth Warren explained the feminist dilemma on March 5, 2020, when she dropped out of the presidential primaries.

> Gender in this race, you know, that is the trap question for every woman. If you say, "yeah, there was sexism in this race," everyone says "whiner," and if you say, "no, there was no sexism," about a bazillion women think, "what planet does she live on."[165]

Now the first woman serves as vice president of the United States, yet an acquaintance, fully in support of women in this role, remarked that he thought Kamala Harris was *lucky* to have a husband

---

[165] Elizabeth Warren, interview by NBC, March 5, 2020, https://www.nbcnews.com/politics/2020-election/elizabeth-warren-reflects-sexism-2020-campaign-after-exiting-race-n1150741.

who supports her as vice president. He did not comment on Joe Biden's luck in having Dr. Jill Biden as a wife. Norms are still deeply embedded in our thinking about the roles of men and women. We watch with interest how Harris is treated and viewed, not just as our vice president but as the first woman in this role. Supreme Court Justice Ruth Bader Ginsberg believed that small steps, one at a time, are needed to make progress for true equality. Harris has taken one small step for woman, one giant leap for womankind.

Should we still use the term *feminism*? It triggers high reactions in many people. Feminists are considered radical, antifamily, obnoxious at worst, and inspiring, empowering, and justice-seeking at best. Is there a better label for those who are determined to achieve political and economic equality for women? Maybe something more neutral like "equal all" or "equal rights activists." Language uplifts us, sometimes splits us, but always defines us.

When I ask my acquaintances if they believe in equal rights for women and men, all say they do. But when I ask my acquaintances if they are feminists, there is a disconnect. Answers begin with, "Yes, but." Women often capitulate: "Yes, but not the kind of woman who is strident and unpleasant," or "Yes, but not the bra burner type," or "Yes, but not the kind who hate men," or "Yes, but I like to be treated like a lady."

Men evade: "Yes, but I still think I should open a door for women," or "Yes, but I don't think women belong on the front lines in combat," or "Yes, but I think men and women are different," or "Yes, but I think we have equality now, so I don't get why there is much of an issue."

Melinda Gates summarizes the ambivalence that exists about feminism. When she was asked if she were a feminist, she said,

> I didn't know what to say. I'm not sure I knew then what a feminist was. That was when our daughter was a little less than a year old. Twenty-two years later, I am an ardent feminist. To me, it's very simple. Being a feminist means believing that every woman should be able to use her voice

and pursue her potential, and that women and men should all work together to take down the barriers and end the biases that still hold women back.[166]

Uncertainty defines our feelings about feminism. Four in ten Americans see the feminist movement as angry, and about the same number feel that men are unfairly blamed for women's challenges.[167] While it seems counterintuitive, women have often been known to fight the most fiercely to prevent women from gaining rights that would benefit them. Throughout time, women have chosen leadership roles in organizations that worked against women's equality.

First-wave anti-feminists

Anti-feminists emerged to fight against the first-wave efforts for women to achieve the vote. The first antisuffrage group in the United States led by a woman was the Anti-Sixteenth Amendment Society, formed in 1868 and supported by more women than men. Madeleine Vinton Dahlgren and her followers believed that women were equal to men but in a different sphere: that of home and motherhood. They wanted politics and the burden of voting to be left to men because women had enough work on their plates with home management, children's education, and entertainment.

The group printed an antisuffrage petition in *Godey's Lady's Book* magazine, which they used to collect five thousand signatures to present to Congress in February 1871.[168] Women authors joined the antisuffrage movement, including Ida Tarbell, a famous, successful woman who had an outstanding career in journalism. In her book *The Business of Being a Woman* (1912), she opined that women were

---

[166] Gates, *The Moment of Lift*, 7.

[167] Weiyi Cal and Scott Clement, "What Americans Think About Feminism Today," *The Washington Post*, January 27, 2016, https://www.washingtonpost.com/graphics/national/feminism-project/poll/.

[168] Elizabeth Cady Stanton, Susan Anthony, and Matilda Gage, *History of Woman Suffrage*, vol. 3 (Fowler and Well, 1861–1876), 494–495.

incapable of achieving what men could and that a woman's place was in the home. Paula Treckel, professor emerita of history at Allegheny College, said in a lecture in 1997,

> This woman, [Tarbell] who personified the word "success" in her own generation, and who, if she were alive today, would stand at the forefront of journalism, was the same woman who asserted that women's place was in the home and that they were incapable of greatness in a man's world because of their nature.[169]

Tarbell was unable to break free of norms that shackled her even when they were contradictory to her own life.

My grandmother was born in 1878 and lived most of her life in North Dakota. There, she witnessed the march down the hard path of securing the right for women to vote. North Dakota men and women argued that if women gained the right to vote, wives might neglect their husbands and become corrupted. They believed that a woman should not be involved in politics because that was men's work. Still, others were undaunted and aligned with and supported the suffragettes.

The Votes for Women League was organized in 1912 with chapters in Fargo and Grand Forks, North Dakota. In 1913, when my grandmother was thirty-five years old, a bill that allowed women to vote was supported by Votes for Women League and passed in both houses of the North Dakota legislation. The bill was placed on the ballot for the 1914 state general election, and *men* voted on whether *women* should have the right to vote in the next election. Two groups, the Anti-Woman Suffrage League and the Association Opposed to Women Suffrage, backed by the railroad and liquor industries, worked strenuously to prevent North Dakota women from voting.

---

[169] Paula Treckel, "Ida Tarbell and the Business of Being a Woman," 1997.

Neither Republican nor Democratic parties supported the suffrage bill, and the question failed by about nine thousand votes, locking women in North Dakota out of the vote. Suffrage bills were reintroduced in the North Dakota legislation in 1915 and 1917 with the support of the Nonpartisan League (NPL). Finally, a bill passed that gave limited voting rights to women on county and city issues, but it did not allow women to vote in national elections for North Dakota senators or representatives to Congress.

A suffrage amendment was introduced in Congress in 1878 and did not pass in the house until June 4, 1919, over forty years later. The bill passed in the Senate soon after with overwhelming Republican support. Then the bill moved to state-by-state votes with three-fourths (thirty-six) of the states needed for ratification. The North Dakota legislature ratified the Nineteenth Amendment on December 1, 1919. Tennessee, the needed thirty-sixth state, ratified the amendment eight months later on August 18, 1920. Two days later, on August 20, 1920, the US Congress passed the Nineteenth Amendment, granting full suffrage to women while voices of women in the balcony sang the Christian doxology, "Praise God from Whom All Blessings Flow." Church bells rang out across North Dakota in support of women being given a voice in our country's future. My grandmother, at age forty-two, had fully gained the right to vote.[170]

This milestone for women did not include a milestone for women of color. Barriers were set in place that prevented women of color from voting fully until the Voting Rights Act of 1965, which outlawed discriminatory practices like literacy tests.

Second-wave anti-feminists

Second-wave anti-feminists held the same views as a first wave antisuffrage groups: a woman's place is in the home. Second-wave anti-feminists were trolling for a new target. They found the tar-

---

[170] North Dakota Studies. State Historical Society of North Dakota. Unit III: Waves of Development (1861–1920). Lesson 4: Alliances and Conflicts. Topic 8: Suffrage.

get in the Twenty-Seventh Amendment, known as the Equal Rights Amendment (ERA) passed in both the US Senate and the house of representatives in 1972. Congress required three-fourths (thirty-eight) of the states to ratify the ERA by 1979. Support was high for the bill, and over one hundred thousand people participated in the March for the Equal Rights Amendment in 1978. Twenty-two states ratified the ERA in the first year.

A Harris poll administered between 1971 and 1975 assessed the level of agreement with efforts to strengthen and change a women's status in society. During this four-year period, support for women grew seventeen percentage points from 42 percent in 1971 to 59 percent in 1975, the fastest rate of support for women of any time.[171] The passage of the ERA looked to be a sure thing.

The ERA hit a brick wall built by Phyllis Schlafly, a conservative political activist from Alton, Illinois. Schlafly was one of the most polarizing anti-feminists of her time. She gained fame through her self-published book *A Choice Not an Echo: The Inside Story of How American Presidents Are Chosen*, which supported Barry Goldwater's 1964 presidential run. With a good understanding of political systems and a needed outlet for her leadership talent, Schlafly organized a grassroots movement, STOP ERA (Stop Taking Our Privileges) and started the Eagle Forum newsletter to defeat the ratification of ERA. She asserted that women were already protected, and ratification of the ERA would end women's protection and privileges if equality were granted under the law. At the time, she was a member of the John Birch Society, a far-right organization that opposed the Civil Rights Act of 1964, communism, the redistribution of wealth, and immigration. The John Birch Society also was rife with conspiracy theories, claiming that President Eisenhower was a communist and that Joe McCarthy had been murdered by communists.

---

[171] "Two in Three Americans Favor Enhancing Women's Status in Society," The Harris Poll, March 10, 2017, https://theharrispoll.com/as-americans-took-part-in-international-womens-day-a-collective-day-of-global-celebration-and-a-call-for-gender-parity-a-new-harris-poll-finds-that-two-in-three-americans-66-say-they-favo/.

In the Eagle Forum newsletter "What's Wrong with Equal Rights for Women," Schlafly claimed that the passage of the ERA would lead to "Government-funded abortions, homosexual school-teachers, women forced into military service, and men refusing to support their wives."[172] She campaigned in various states on the stand that the ERA would take away a woman's right to be a homemaker and mother as well as other untruths. Schlafly was an effective speaker and skillful at forging conservative political alliances that championed family values and traditional gender roles. In 1975, STOP ERA was renamed Eagle Forum.

The next, year the GOP national platform first used the term "family values." The platform stated,

> It is imperative that our government's programs, actions, officials and social welfare institutions never be allowed to jeopardize the family. We fear the government may be powerful enough to destroy our families.[173]

A year later, at the National Women's Conference in Houston, Texas, Schlafly branded feminists efforts at passing the ERA as "anti-family."

The GOP positioned the government and the family as political enemies. Government-provided day care centers were suspected of molding children's minds. Public schools were attacked by conservatives for teaching liberal thinking. Universities were accused of promoting antiauthority and antireligious ideology. Textbook battles broke out nationally, and parents became impassioned about who should teach children and what they should be taught. Homeschool became a strategy to avoid the public schools' antifamily curriculum. Educational programs like outcome-based education, whole language, and Common Core came under constant criticism as conservatives used disinformation to undermine them. Books deemed too

---

[172] "Eagle Forum," *Wikipedia*.
[173] The Harris Poll.

liberal were banned, sex education should be taught by the family, and evolution was not the Bible's version of the creation of man. Today, we see the same concerns from conservatives. Teaching about evolution, critical race theory and LGBTQ+ are examples of curriculum considered inappropriate by conservative groups.

Second-wave anti-feminists, religious white Evangelicals, and the GOP found common ground on the issue of family values. They feared that traditional gender roles and sexual norms were disintegrating. A campaign on saving family values was launched. The ideal family was defined as headed by a wage-earning cis husband with a cis wife who managed the home and children. Homosexuality, divorce, Planned Parenthood, civil unions, transgender people, and abortion were considered antifamily. The political scene was set to take on the Equal Rights Amendment (ERA), which anti-feminists identified as the single biggest threat to family values.

Persuasive arguments about how women would lose cherished family values eclipsed evidence to the contrary. Several of my acquaintances during this time were persuaded by Schlafly's rhetoric and feared that men and women would need to share bathrooms and that women would lose the right to stay home and raise a family if they chose. Ironically, these same acquaintances were teachers already balancing children and careers.

The powerful message from the right insured that enough states could not be won over by the first ERA deadline, and it was extended to 1982. The required thirty-eighth state was not reached by the 1982 deadline and hopes for passage of the ERA faded away.

Historian Judith Glazer-Raymo stated,

> As moderates, we thought we represented the forces of reason and goodwill but failed to take seriously the power of the family values argument and the single-mindedness of Schlafly and her followers. The ERA's defeat seriously damaged the women's movement, destroying its momentum and its potential to foment social change... Eventually, this resulted in feminist dissatisfaction

with the Republican Party, giving the Democrats
a new source of strength.[174]

Critics of Schlafly were bemused as she advocated for other
women to be full-time wives and mothers while she herself was a
lawyer, an editor, and a political activist who ran for several political positions in Illinois. She successfully opposed the radical feminist movement, and in a ten-year battle, she was victorious as the
time limit ran out for the ERA's ratification. She was instrumental in
defining feminists as antifamily. She died in 2016, two years before
her home state, Illinois, ratified the ERA in 2018 and thirty-six years
after its passage in Congress. Too late, in 2020, the ERA eventually
gained ratification of the needed thirty-eight states. The ERA, proposed by Alice Paul in 1923 nearly one hundred years ago, never
became law for women.

Many credit Schlafly's success of the Eagle Forum as instrumental in shifting the GOP further right. She effectively aligned the
GOP platform with conservative Christianity and far-right ideology. This platform did not support abortion, gun control, or gay
rights. Ironically, Schlafly's son John, forty-one, confirmed he was
gay in 1992, yet he stood at his mother's side at the 2004 Republican
National Convention, where she advocated for a constitutional
ban on same-sex marriage. Schlafly damaged women's progress for
equality by persuading women to vote against their own best interests. Conservative and Evangelical women continued to strengthen
anti-feminist alliances. An unintended consequence of the ERA fight
was that moderate women moved to the Democratic Party and,
combined with minorities, played a significant role in electing Bill
Clinton to the presidency.

Another famous anti-feminist of the 1970s and '80s was Anita
Bryant, a popular singer, former Miss Oklahoma, and fundamen-
talist Christian who believed homosexuality was sinful and against
God's will. In 1969, she became a spokesperson for the Florida Citrus

---

[174] Judith Glazer-Raymo, *Shattering the Myths: Women in Academe* (Baltmore and
London: Johns Hopkins University Press, 2001), 19.

Commission. She sang her way into our homes through national TV, promoting Tropicana orange juice.

In 1977, Dade County, Florida, passed an antidiscrimination ordinance on the basis of sexual orientation. Bryant used her fame to spearhead the first national organized opposition to gay rights when she became the leader of the coalition Save Our Children with the goal of repealing the Dade County antidiscrimination ordinance. *Newsweek* magazine reported that the organization took out full-page ads warning that gay and lesbian lifestyle was a "hair-raising pattern of recruitment and outright seductions and molestations" of children.[175] Her campaign successfully led to the 1977 repeal of the antidiscriminatory ordinance.

In Dade County, Florida, legislators also approved a law prohibiting gay and lesbian adoption, which was not repealed until November 25, 2008, when it was declared unconstitutional.[176] Bryant went on to campaign against other gay antidiscrimination laws in Minnesota, Oregon, Kansas, and California.

Backlash followed. A boycott of orange juice saw gay bars replace the screwdriver, a cocktail made with vodka and orange juice, with the Anita Bryant Cocktail, made with vodka and apple juice. Celebrities and other gay rights sympathizers joined the push back against Bryant. When the Texas Bar Association invited Bryant to perform in Houston, Texas, thousands of gay supporters marched in protest on June 16, 1977. This became a turning point in the fight for gay rights.

Bryant's proposed TV weekly variety series was cancelled by Tele-Tactics, a New York television production firm. Barry Drucker, president, said in a telegram,

> We sincerely regret that the extensive national
> publicity arising from the controversial political

---

[175] "No to Gays," *Newsweek*, June 20, 1977, 27–29.
[176] Yolanne Almanzar, "Florida Gay Adoption Ban Is Ruled Unconstitutional," *The New York Times*, November 25, 2008, https://www.nytimes.com/2008/11/26/us/26florida.html.

activities you have been engaged in Dade County prohibit us from utilizing your services.[177]

Eventually, her contract with Tropicana was not renewed. She and her husband divorced and her conservative support, which did not support divorce, fell away. Because of her fight against homosexuality, Bryant suffered the unanticipated consequence of launching the gay rights movement in the United States and eventually cementing support for nondiscrimination laws for the LGBTQI+ community.

Modern day anti-feminists still seek to preserve traditional roles of men and women as natural and beneficial to society while continuing to paint feminists as antifamily. Rush Limbaugh, who was awarded with the Presidential Medal of Freedom by President Trump in 2020, vilified the definition of feminist. In his book *The Way Things Ought to Be* (1992), Limbaugh used the word *feminazi* to describe women who held different views from his. He said,

> A feminazi is a woman to whom the most important thing in life is seeing to it that as many abortions as possible are performed… Feminazis have adopted abortion as a kind of sacrament for their religion/politics of alienation and bitterness.[178]

The reference to Nazi equated abortions to the holocaust, suggesting that ending life was the goal of women who wanted reproductive rights. Cementing feminists as man-haters—and in this case, baby-haters—became a theme with anti-feminists.

---

[177] Jay Clarke, "Gay Rights Dispute Stops Bryant's Show," *The Washington Post*, February 25, 1977, https://www.washingtonpost.com/archive/politics/1977/03/27/gay-rights-fight-shaping-up-in-miami/e4f596c1-f8e0-4785-b528-599077a478ba/.

[178] Rush Limbaugh, *The Way Thing Ought to Be* (Pocket Books, 1992), 194–195.

Candace Owens is a prominent far-right commentator and director of communications at the conservative advocacy group Turning Point USA. On September 9, 2019, she tweeted,

> Modern feminism—which has absolutely nothing to do with earlier feminism—is an abomination. It's goal is to remove all traces of masculinity from the western world and in the process, breakdown the family unit. If manhood becomes obsolete, so too will the families.[179]

Generations of feminists have paved the way for Owens to choose to work as a profession or be in her home. Her takeaway is that feminists' goal is not about equality but rather to diminish men and reverse the patriarchal order, establishing men subordinate to women.

Laura Ingraham and Ann Coulter, two far-right Fox News commentators, use their national platform to denigrate feminists' efforts. Ingraham founded the far-right news website LifeZette. She was also a member of the Independent Women's Forum (IWF), a group that supported Clarence Thomas's appointment to the Supreme Court by discrediting Anita Hill. The IWF recently opposed National Pay Inequity Awareness Day, suggesting that shining a light on wage discrimination causes girls and women to think of themselves as victims. They also opposed sexual harassment training because they believed women's claims were often made up or exaggerated, and sexual harassment training encourages people to see the worst in each other. Ingraham opposed the Violence Against Women Act, asserting the bill had a tear-jerking title and that women who marry are safer than women who are not married.[180] This conclusion is the same

---

[179] Candance Owens (@RealCandanceO), Twitter, September 19, 2019.

[180] Christina Cauterucci, "Laura Ingraham Has Deep Ties to an Anti-Feminist Group That Pooh-Poohs Claims of Sexual Harassment," Slate, August 31, 2017, https://slate.com/human-interest/2017/08/laura-ingraham-has-deep-ties-to-an-anti-feminist-group-that-pooh-poohs-claims-of-sexual-harassment.html.

as that of anti-feminists in the eighteenth and nineteenth centuries: women need to marry and be under the protection of their husbands.

Coulter was asked to author an article for Moneyish to mark Equal Pay Day in 2017. She began by saying, "I'll happily take sixty-nine cents on the dollar, or whatever the feminist myth is nowadays, if I never have to pay for dinner." This comment is surely that of a rich woman who *can* afford to take sixty-nine cents on the dollar.

According to Coulter, sexism is "mostly a comforting excuse." She further dismissed claims of pay inequality, explaining, "As one famous man said, when you're rich, women will let you do ANYTHNG. That's why men are generally more willing to put in horrendous hours and work crap jobs than women are."[181]

Coulter's celebration of a famous rich man, of course, refers to Donald Trump. In a secret recording released by *The Washington Post*, Trump, caught on a hot mic, says,

> I did try and fuck her. She was married. I moved on her very heavily... I moved on her like I was a bitch. Then all of a sudden, I see her. She's now got the big phony tits and everything.

Trump added that he might use some breath mints because...

> I'm automatically attracted to beautiful—I just start kissing them. It's like a magnet. Just kiss. I don't even wait. When you're a star, they let you do it. You can do anything. Grab 'em by the pussy. You can do anything.[182]

---

[181] Ann Coulter, "Equal Pay Day: Ann Coulter Says 'I'll Happily Take 69 Cents on the Dollar, if I Never Have to Pay for Dinner,'" *Marketwatch*, April 4, 2017, https://www.marketwatch.com/story/equal-pay-day-ann-coulter-says-ill-happily-take-69-cents-on-the-dollar-if-i-never-have-to-pay-for-dinner-2017-04-04-1188377.

[182] Libby Nelson, "'Grab 'Em by the Pussy': How Trump Talked about Women in Private Is Horrifying," *Vox*, October 7, 2016, https://www.vox.com/2016/10/7/13205842/trump-secret-recording-women.

Far-right conservatives and Evangelicals dismissed his comments as no big deal, just locker-room boy talk. They justified supporting a man who demeans women by saying that while they don't like what Trump says, they love what he has done for the country.

In 2018, British broadcaster Piers Morgan interviewed then President Donald Trump and asked if he was a feminist. Trump said, "I wouldn't say I'm a feminist—I mean, I think that would be, maybe, going too far."[183] Trump, like many other right leaning world leaders, sees little value in the skills that women bring to leadership.

Robert Fisher, a Republican state representative from New Hampshire, presented a similar dismissal of women. He resigned after his 2019 comments about women came to light on Reddit forum *The Red Pill*. Under a false username, he said that women were "lackluster and boring, serving little purpose in day-to-day life." He also suggested that they should keep a log of their sexual activity to avoid false rape allegations.[184]

The Republican brand touts family values. Although, approving of a man making moves on a married woman and bragging about grabbing women by the pussy seems a long way from both family and values.

The Eagle Forum still exists. The website banner reads, "Eagle Forum: Leading the pro-family movement since 1972." During the pandemic, it displayed a prominent message that read, "STOP COVID-19 Mandatory Vaccination (sign the petition)." The information listed in the Future of the Eagle Forum stated that "President Trump will be successful in advancing other Eagle Forum Causes."[185] One of their causes is taking an antiabortion stand.

Another anti-feminist group led by and supported by women is Women Against Feminism (#WomenAgainstFeminism), which accepts supporter submissions and then solicits readers' comments.

---

[183] Caroline Kenny, "Trump: 'I Wouldn't Say I'm a Feminist,'" CNN, January 29, 2018, https://www.cnn.com/2018/01/28/politics/president-trump-not-feminist-piers-morgan-interview/index.html.

[184] Helen Lewis, "To Learn about the Far Right, Start with the Manosphere," *The Atlantic*, August 7, 2019.

[185] "What Is the Future of the Eagle Forum?" EagleForum.org, January 4, 2021.

A recent article on their website was titled, "3 Reasons Why Women Should Not Vote" (#WhyWomenShouldNotVote). The author admitted that the hashtag started out as a joke, but he changed his mind after he received a large number of responses in favor of his hashtag. Now he agrees with his original assertion that women should not be allowed to vote. The responses to his submission ranged from "women have smaller brains" to "women are too emotional and can't think clearly" to "the Bible says women should have no role in governance."

Historically, women have faced off with each other about equality. Political affiliation strongly affects their views. In 2017, almost three-fourths (74 percent) of female Democrats said that work still needed to be done on gender equality, while only one third (33 percent) of female Republicans agreed. On the other end of the spectrum, female Democrats (4 percent) and female Republicans (14 percent) were more in agreement with the notion that gender equality has gone too far.[186]

Progress is difficult when each step forward is countered by a backward pull. Republican Josh Hawley was a keynote speaker at the National Conservatism Conference in Orlando, Florida, on October 31, 2021. His speech was "The Future of the American Man." In it, he talked about *manhood* and said that he opposes feminism. He believes men are under attack, and consequently,

> Men are withdrawing into the enclave of idleness and pornography and video games. While the left might celebrate this decline of men, I for one cannot join them.[187]

---

[186] "Wide Partisan Gaps in U.S. Over How Far the Country Has Come on Gender Equality," Pew Research Center, October 18, 2017, https://www.pewresearch.org/social-trends/2017/10/18/wide-partisan-gaps-in-u-s-over-how-far-the-country-has-come-on-gender-equality/.

[187] Adam Gabbatt, "Republican Senator Josh Hawley Worries Feminism Has Driven Men to Pornography and Video Games," *The Guardian*, November 1, 2021.

Hawley believes there is a sinister plot devised by feminists to put their feet on men's necks. The opposite is true. All people need to be supported and be equal in the eyes of the law and of society. When any person or group of people—men, women, transgender people, gays, lesbians, nonwhite ethnicities, religions different from Christianity—are singled out and discriminated against, the fabric that makes the up the beautiful quilt of America stretches only over a very few.

When women inexplicably stand in the way of other women's progress, the phenomenon is even more baffling. Dr. Nicole Hemmer summarizes,

> The irony—and really, the tragedy—of female anti-feminists is that their activism increases their own vulnerability. That is not something to be mocked. It is something to be mourned.[188]

Today, we fight too many battles against those with whom we should work together. As the old American saying goes, we circle the wagons and shoot each other. When we strive for equality and fairness to all, we make our country stronger. Together, we can overcome prejudice, hate, and inequality.

[188] Nicole Hemmer, "Anti-Feminist Women Have a Long History in the United States." United States Studies Centre, May 20, 2019, https://www.ussc.edu.au/analysis/anti-feminist-women-have-a-long-history-in-the-united-states.

CHAPTER 10

And Justice for All

> We know that the multiple impacts of COVID-19 have triggered a "shadow pandemic" of increased reported violence of all kinds against women and girls. Every government should be taking strong, proactive steps to address this.
> —Phumzile Mlambo-Ngcuka,
> executive director, UN Women 2021

Every day, millions of US public school children place hands on hearts and recite the Pledge of Allegiance. The pledge is said before sporting events, service club meetings, citizenship ceremonies, congressional meetings, school board meetings, and wherever people wish to say it. We commit loyalty, as a nation, to the values of "liberty and justice for all." Our words assume a deep understanding of and commitment to justice.

Woman Up! focuses primarily on women's equity and justice in the United States. This chapter expands the view to include women throughout the world as we point our lens on gender-based violence. Our global interconnectedness requires an examination of the entirety of womankind when we discuss violence. Women and girls need justice everywhere to survive and thrive.

In June 2020, the United Nations reported that 140 million girls are believed to be *missing* worldwide because of preferences for sons over daughters. Gendercide is the practice of sex selection by aborting, abandoning, neglecting, or killing daughters to increase chances for families to have sons. Young girls may suffer harm once a son is born because his health and welfare matter more to his family than hers. The UNFPA (United Nations Population Foundation) calls this practice "a symptom of entrenched gender inequality" that results in gender imbalance.[189]

Since the 1990s, gender-biased sex selection has resulted in some areas of the world having 25 percent fewer female births than male births. Gender imbalance is further perpetuated when sex selection results in fewer women being available for men to find life partners and raise families. When men eventually find women to marry, boy children are preferred, perpetuating gender imbalance to the next generations. The lack of women life partners exacerbates the cycle of violence as women are kidnapped, forced into child marriages, and become victims of sex trafficking.

In March 2017, the UNFPA, funded by the European Union, launched the Global Programme to Prevent Son Preference and the Undervaluing of Girls, which is the first global initiative of its kind. They plan to team with governments and local partners to gather data about sex ratios in Asia and the Caucasus. They believe this is key to addressing the problem of girls' low value and bringing about lasting change for women's human rights.[190]

Sex selection in the US is legal, and it is big business. People from other countries travel to the US to take advantage of sophisticated technology to select the preferred sex of their child. American men show preference for sons to daughters by a 43 percent to 24 percent margin according to a 2018 Gallup poll. Women showed no sex preference.[191]

---

[189] The Associated Press, "UN says 140 million females 'missing' due to son preference," ABC News, June 30, 2020, https://abcnews.go.com/US/wireStory/140-million-females-missing-due-son-preference-71547237.

[190] "Gender-Biased Sex Selection," United Nations Population Fund, https://www.unfpa.org/gender-biased-sex-selection.

[191] Frank Newport, "Slight Preference for Having Boy Children Persists in U.S.," *Gallup*, July 5, 2018, https://news.gallup.com/poll/236513/slight-preference-having-boy-children-persists.aspx.

The largest study of violence against women was conducted in 2021 by the World Health Organization (WHO) on behalf of the United Nations. The data show that "violence against women remains devastatingly pervasive and starts alarmingly young."[192] About one in three women throughout the world are subjected to sexual or physical violence in their lifetime. In the United States, the number is about one in four. Those numbers have remained largely unchanged over the past decade, with younger women more at risk than older women.

WHO Director General Dr. Tedros Adhanom Ghebreyesus said in the same report,

> We can only fight it with deep-rooted and sustained efforts—by governments, communities and individuals—to change harmful attitudes, improve access to opportunities and services for women and girls, and foster healthy and mutually respectful relationships.

The WHO report states that violence against women can be prevented. It recommends gender transformative policies for women around childcare, equal pay, and laws that support gender equality.

While WHO called on governments to lead the way in preventing violence against women, US House Minority Leader Kevin McCarthy said at a 2021 GOP fundraising dinner that "it will be hard not to hit Pelosi with a gavel if I become Speaker of the House."[193] Former US President Donald Trump said, "When you're a star—you can do anything. Grab 'em by the pussy. You can do anything."[194] Abuse against women is a joking matter for some government lead-

---

[192] Joint News Release, Geneva/New York, March 9, 2021, https://who.canto.global/b/QR99R.

[193] Daniella Diaz, Nicky Robertson, and Chandelis Duster, "McCarthy Says 'It Will Be Hard Not to Hit' Pelosi with Gavel if He Becomes House Speaker," CNN, August 2, 2021, https://www.cnn.com/2021/08/01/politics/kevin-mccarthy-nancy-pelosi-gavel/index.html.

[194] Libby.

ers. In November 2021, Representative Paul Gosar, Arizona, posted an altered video of him killing Representative Alexandria Ocasio-Cortez while asking, "Any fans out there?"[195] Violent words thrown around by powerful men have serious consequences.

Within days of the WHO report, eight women were massacred in spas in Atlanta, Georgia, on March 21, 2021. Six were Asian. The initial motive given by the killer was his sexual addiction. Asian women have long been portrayed in the media as linked to sex work and as submissive and sexually desirable. Asian women have been stereotyped for years, with little attention given to calling out this discrimination. The history of violence against Asians in the US is deeply rooted. This issue is finally gaining the some of the attention it deserves.

A spike in verbal and physical violence against Asians has occurred since the pandemic, fueled in part by President Trump's racial characterization of COVID-19 as "kung-flu" and the "China virus." The FBI reports that anti-Asian hate crimes increased by 73 percent in 2020, with white people making up the largest number of offenders.

In addition to the pandemic fueling hatred, Chinese-US relations deteriorated, causing some people in the US to question the loyalty of Asian Americans. This long-standing attitude harkens back to the United States internment of Japanese during World War II. The Stop AAPI Hate national report states from March 19, 2020, to September 30, 2021, a total of 10,370 hate incidents have occurred against Asian American and Pacific Islander. Nearly one in five AAPI people have experienced a hate crime in the past year. Harassment and avoidance or shunning make up the greatest number of violations, followed by physical assault and online misconduct. Hate crimes against women make up 62 percent of all reports. These num-

---

[195] Rachel Treisman, "Rep. Paul Gosar Shared an Anime Video of Himself Killing AOC. This Was Her Response," NPR, November 9, 2021, https://www.npr.org/2021/11/09/1053895408/paul-gosar-alexandria-ocasio-cortez-anime-twitter-video-backlash.

bers are likely underreported.[196] #StopAsianHate is one example of nonprofits that have formed in response to rising hate crimes against Asians.

The COVID-19 Hate Crimes Act was proposed by Hawaii senator Mazie Hirono in April 2021. After changes to the language, including references to COVID-19, the bill passed the Senate with bipartisan support. Speaking from the senate floor, Hirono exclaimed,

> We sent a powerful message of solidarity to the AAPI community that the Senate won't be a bystander as anti-Asian violence surges in our country.[197]

The Violence Against Women Act (VAWA) provided resources for victims of domestic violence and sexual assault. It was signed into law in 1993 and expired in 2018. Since then, Congress has not reauthorized the act. In March 2021, the US house of representatives passed the reauthorization of the law by 244 votes (215 Democrat, twenty-nine Republican) with all 172 no votes cast by Republicans.[198] The vote in the Senate has been held up because Republicans have issues with certain expansions of the bill, primarily a gun-purchasing provision that increases the threshold for those with misdemeanor convictions of domestic abuse or stalking. Republicans also reject how the proposed law closes the "boyfriend loophole" that expands the definition of abusers to include dating partners that would limit their access to buy guns.

[196] Aggie Yellow Horse, Russell Jeung, and Ronae Matriano, "Stop AAPI Hate National Report," March 19, 2020, and September 30, 2021, https://stopaapihate.org/wp-content/uploads/2021/11/21-SAH-NationalReport2-v2.pdf.

[197] Savannah Behrmann, "COVID-19 Hate Crimes Bill to Fight Asian American Discrimination Passes Senate," *USA Today*, April 22, 2021, https://iwpr.org/iwpr-issues/race-ethnicity-gender-and-economy/violence-against-black-women-many-types-far-reaching-effects/.

[198] James Walker, "Full List of 172 Republicans Who Opposed the Violence Against Women Act," *Newsweek*, March 18, 2021, https://www.newsweek.com/full-list-172-republicans-opposed-violence-against-women-act-1577029.

Violence against ethnic and nonconforming women in the US is widespread and disproportionally higher than violence against white cis women. Black women are more likely to be raped, expelled, or suspended from school, and they suffer from police brutality more than other women overall.[199] The 2015 Violence Policy Center reported that Black women in the US are more likely to be murdered at two and a half times the rate of white women and almost always by someone they know.[200]

American Indian women and native Alaskan women suffer the highest rates of assault and domestic violence of any US ethnic group. More than 84 percent experience violence in their lifetime. The occurrences are likely underreported because they fear retribution from their offenders, and they live in isolated areas with a lack of resources, including law enforcement.[201]

Fatal violence against the transgender and gender nonconforming community was the highest in 2020 since the Human Rights Campaign (HRC) began keeping records in 2013. The majority of these victims were Black and Latinx transgender women.[202]

Gender-based violence takes many forms. Sex trafficking accounts for more than four million victims globally, and 99 percent are women and girls.[203] In the United States, illicit massage parlors with ties to sex trafficking are a multibillion-dollar industry, where

[199] Susan Green, "Violence Against Black Women—Many Types, Far-reaching Effects," Institute for Women's Policy Research, August 20, 2020, https://iwpr.org/iwpr-issues/race-ethnicity-gender-and-economy/violence-against-black-women-many-types-far-reaching-effects/.

[200] "Study Finds Black Women Murdered by Men Are Nearly Always Killed by Someone They Know, Most Commonly with a Gun," Violence Policy Center, September 21, 2017, https://vpc.org/press/study-finds-black-women-murdered-by-men-are-nearly-always-killed-by-someone-they-know-most-commonly-with-a-gun-3/.

[201] The National Coalition Against Domestic Violence, https://ncady.org/stattistics.

[202] "Fatal Violence Against the Transgender and Gender Non-Conforming Community in 2021," HRC, https://www.hrc.org/resources/fatal-violence-against-the-transgender-and-gender-non-conforming-community-in-2021.

[203] Cara Kelly, "13 Sex Trafficking Statistics that Explain the Enormity of the Global Sex Trade," USA Today, July 30, 2019, https://www.usatoday.com/story/

women are forced into sex labor. The US does not specifically keep sex trafficking numbers. These data should be a part of a national crime base in order to have a better understanding of the magnitude of the problem. The majority of forced-sex workers in the US are from China, followed by South Korea. Runaway children and girls in foster care are particularly vulnerable to trafficking.[204]

Polaris, founded in 2002, serves victims of human trafficking, collects data, and uses strategies to disrupt trafficking in the US. Polaris's National Human Trafficking Hotline received reports of 34,700 situations of sex trafficking between 2007 and 2017. Incredibly, in 2019 alone, 11,500 situations of human trafficking were reported to the hotline. The website adds that as shocking as these numbers are, they are likely only a fraction of the actual problem.[205]

According to the NCADV (National Coalition Against Domestic Violence), more than ten million women and men in the United States experience domestic violence annually, which translates into twenty people per minute.[206] Intimate partner violence (IPV) includes physical violence, sexual violence, stalking, and psychological violence by a romantic partner. One in seven women and one in twenty-five men are injured by an intimate partner.[207] The economic effects of domestic violence are staggering. Domestic violence costs 8.3 billion dollars annually, which represents a combination of lost productivity from work and medical expenses.[208]

More than half of US women have experienced street harassment, such as men shouting harassing or sexually suggestive epi-

---

news/investigations/2019/07/29/12-trafficking-statistics-enormity-global-sex-trade/1755192001/.

[204] Ibid.

[205] PolarisProject.org.

[206] "National Intimate Partner and Sexual Violence Survey," 2010 Summary Report, CDC, https://www.cdc.gov/violenceprevention/pdf/nisvs_report2010-a.pdf.

[207] Ibid.

[208] Robert Pearl, "Domestic Violence: The Secret Killer That Costs $8.3 Billion Annually," *Forbes*, December 5, 2013, https://www.forbes.com/sites/robertpearl/2013/12/05/domestic-violence-the-secret-killer-that-costs-8-3-billion-annually/?sh=5a35b9b24681.

thets, asking for personal information, following, or calling out vile words. Lesbians, bisexual women, and women of color experience street harassment more than other women.[209] While street harassment might sound trivial, it is part of a pervasive pattern of abuse. Perpetrators often see their antics as funny or high jinx, but harassment doesn't feel funny to those on the receiving end.

Often, women have not found their voice against abuse and violence. Sometimes they do. Michael Sanguinetti, a Toronto, Canada, police constable and another officer were addressing the topic of campus rape at a York University safety forum in January 2011. He said, "I've been told not to say this—however, women should avoid dressing like sluts in order not to be victimized." His apology followed.

The term "slut-shaming" was quickly transformed into a national protest movement: SlutWalk.[210] The first SlutWalk took place in Toronto, Ontario on April 3, 2011, with over three thousand participants dressed in revealing clothing, high heels, tall boots, and oversize accessories. Many were sex workers who demanded decriminalization. SlutWalk became an international movement aimed at ending rape culture and victim blaming, emphasizing that dressing in a certain way does not excuse harassment or violence. SlutWalks followed in the United States, Australia, Germany, the United Kingdom, Israel, and the Netherlands as well as in Latin America and Asia between 2011 and 2020.

Women's attire also played a role in a study published in the *Journal of Vascular Surgery* that attempted to analyze the behavior of trainees in vascular surgery. The research team created fake posts to observe trainees and determine if they were *professional* or *unprofessional*. Among the definition of unprofessional was "inappropriate attire." Researchers defined women doctors as *unprofessional* because they posted pictures of themselves in their private lives wearing swimsuits and Halloween costumes that the researchers deemed too provocative.

---

[209] "Preventing Intimate Partner Violence. Centers for Disease Control and Prevention," CDC, https://www.cdc.gov/violenceprevention/intimatepartnerviolence/fastfact.html.

[210] "Slutwalk," *Wikipedia*.

The response to the published article was #MedBikini. On July 23, 2020, female physicians around the world began posting pictures of themselves in swimsuits. Many male physicians joined in and posted pictures of themselves in swimsuits to support their female colleagues. Eventually, the journal article was retracted, and the authors apologized. Writers Arghavan Salles and Rena Malik noted,

> The point is not who these researchers are or even what they did in this particular study. The authors, the institutional review board (which is supposed to watch out for ethical problems), the reviewers of the article, and the journal's editors all thought this was worth publishing. This is because in the culture of medicine, harassment and subjugation of those who don't look like the dominant group is not only tolerated, it's the norm.[211]

The Global Gender Gap Index from the World Economic Forum uses four measures to determine progress in closing the gender gap: (1) economic participation and opportunity, (2) educational attainment, (3) health and survival, and (4) political empowerment. Saadia Zahidi, managing director of the World Economic Forum, said that the US had gone backward in gender equality in the decade between 2006 and 2016. On the political equality index, the US fell in rank from sixty-sixth place to seventy-third place, and economic gender equality declined from third place to twenty-sixth in the same decade. Zahidi stated that no matter who was elected president in November 2016, he or she would need to make gender equality in America great again.[212]

---

[211] Arghavan Salles and Rena Malik, "Why Doctors Are Posing in Swimwear on Social Media," *Scientific America*, July 28, 2020, https://www.scientificamerican.com/article/why-doctors-are-posing-in-swimwear-on-social-media/.

[212] Saadia Zahidi, "American Is Falling behind Other Countries in Gender Equality. The Next President Must Fix That," World Economic Forum,

The Global Gender Gap Index measures underlying issues that can lead to gender-based violence using a scale of 0 to 100 to indicate what percentage of the gender gap needs to be closed in various countries. The World Economic Forum Global Gender Gap Report 2021 stated that the impact of the COVID-19 pandemic has negatively affected closing the gap. The number of years necessary to close the gender gap has increased globally from 99.5 years to 135.6 years. In North America, the gender gap could be closed in 61.5 years, given a more serious effort for gender equality.[213] The United States ranked fifty-three of 153 countries in gender equality, lower than Zimbabwe. The countries that rank the highest in gender equity are Nordic countries: Iceland, Norway, Finland, and Sweden.[214]

The return of Afghanistan to the Taliban has turned the world's eyes to the plight of women and girls who live under men's harsh rule. When the Taliban was previously in power from 1996 to 2001, girls were forbidden to attend school, learn to read, or appear in public places without a male relative. Women's human rights were part of the justification for the US decision to invade Afghanistan after 9/11 in 2001. First Lady Laura Bush said as the Taliban was retreating, "The people of Afghanistan, especially women, are rejoicing."[215]

Although criticism has been leveled about the extent of the US commitment to girls' and women's rights in Afghanistan over the past twenty years, they did gain access to education, women journalists were trained, women took seats in government, and money and resources were provided to increase their opportunities. The return

---

October 27, 2016, https://www.weforum.org/agenda/2016/10/global-gender-gap-2016-usa-saadia-zahidi/.

[213] "World Economic Forum Global Gender Gap Report 2021," Insight Report, March 3, 2021, https://www.weforum.org/reports/ab6795a1-960c-42b2-b3d5-587eccda6023/digest.

[214] Catherine Thorbecke, "The US Ranked Lower than Zimbabwe for Gender Equality This Year, See How Low It Sank," ABC News (December 17, 2019, https://abcnews.go.com/Business/us-ranked-lower-zimbabwe-gender-equality-year-low/story?id=67775137.

[215] Laura King and Marcus Yam, "The Taliban Is Back—Afghan Women Are Scared, but Defiant," *Los Angeles Times*, November 7, 2021, https://www.latimes.com/projects/afghan-women/.

of Taliban rule and Sharia law sees women and girls losing the progress they had gained. The Taliban indicated that it would govern less harshly than before, granting women more dignity and rights.

To date, the Taliban has been uneven in in its governance. It has stated that women can participate fully in society but only within the rules of Islamic law. They have abolished the Afghan Ministry of Women's Affairs and replaced it with an organization that promotes women's virtue. Naheed Samadi, US country director of Women for Afghan Women, said, "We are back where we started. It is very heart-breaking and very hard." Even when rights are won for girls and women, there is no guarantee that they will endure.

Gender-based violence is rampant around the world. The United Nations estimates that about five thousand women are victims of honor killings every year. Honor killings are nearly always women. They are murdered for having brought shame to their families by violating cultural norms and expectations. Killing cleanses the family's honor. The murderers are generally male family members, although sometimes, children are the perpetrators because they face lesser penalties. Sometimes, honor killings are forced suicides, which escape punishment.

Honor killings persist because of traditions and practices within the culture. In the United States, honor killing exists in immigrant communities. Fauzia Mohammed was stabbed eleven times by her brother in upstate New York because she wore immodest clothes. She survived but forever lives with the knowledge that her family attempted to kill her because she was shameful. Noor Almaleki of Phoenix, Arizona, was killed when her father ran over her in a parking lot. She refused to be forced into marriage by her father with a man who needed a green card. Sarah and Amina Said, seventeen-year-old and eighteen-year-old sisters, were shot to death by their father in Dallas, Texas, for dating American boys. At a vigil in remembrance of the sisters, their brother spoke, saying, "They pulled the trigger, not my dad."[216] His message was that his sisters' deaths were their

---

[216] Ayaan Hirsi Ali, "Honor Killings in America," *The Atlantic*, April 30, 2015, https://www.theatlantic.com/politics/archive/2015/04/honor-killings-in-america/391760/.

own fault, not their fathers, because they didn't live by the rules of the men of the family.

Female genital mutilation (FGM) is the partial or total removal of female external genitalia. There is no medical benefit, and it is usually performed on girls younger than a year to fifteen years old. The UN estimates that two hundred million girls worldwide have been subjected to FGM. The highest incidence is in Africa, with Somalia having the highest rate of FGM with 98 percent of girls having undergone the procedure. Although FGM has been banned, like so many other violent crimes against women, it persists due to social norms.[217]

According to Global Citizen, Honduras is the femicide capital of the world. On average, a woman is murdered every eighteen hours, and 90 percent of perpetrators get away with the crime. The crimes are believed to be related to domestic violence and drug and human trafficking. Honduras is one of the least safe places for women to live.[218]

The recurring theme of violence against women cries out: women's rights are human rights. Often isolated and voiceless, women have grappled with systematic violence, discrimination, and disadvantage throughout time and around the globe. Violence is the dubious birthright of women. Women are predominantly the victims of worldwide sex trafficking, gendercide, genital mutilation, child marriage, honor killings, and rape. Pressure must be exerted to demand that governments keep accurate statistics on crimes committed against women and create and enforce policies that protect women. As long as boys and men are more valued and have more rights than girls and women, the global scales of justice will remain unbalanced.

Addressing the challenges of racism, quality childcare, violence, sexual harassment, attaining leadership positions, discrimination against ethnic and nonconforming women, and equal pay

---

[217] "Eighty Per Cent of FGM Cases Happen in Africa," Relief Web, February 24, 2021, https://reliefweb.int/report/world/eighty-cent-fgm-cases-happen-africa.

[218] Daniele Selby, "5 of the World's Worst Countries for Gender Equality," Global Citizen, July 12, 2016, https://www.globalcitizen.org/es/content/worst-places-woman-yemen-congo-saudi-arabia/.

are only a few issues that will begin to close the gender equity gap. Audre Lorde—self-described Black, lesbian, mother, warrior, poet—declared, "Tomorrow belongs to those of us who conceive of it belonging to everyone: who lend the best of ourselves to it, and with joy."[219]

As we continue to pledge allegiance to our country and to the values in which we believe, we must realize "and justice for all" means inclusion, safety, fairness, and acceptance for every person. The three deadliest words in the world cannot be "it's a girl." We can do better. We can extend a helping hand, give positive support, offer encouragement, and provide resources for all of us to be able to live in a more just and peaceably society. When we uphold all human rights, we lift every woman up.

---

[219] Audre Lorde, *A Burst of Light and Other Essays* (Courier Dover Publications, 2017), 96.

ABOUT THE AUTHOR

Linda Hanson's career spanned fifty years of public school education as an art teacher, principal, superintendent, and a small business owner. She has presented and published nationally on learning and leadership topics. She has a doctorate in education and has won numerous leadership awards.

Linda is married to a composer/symphony conductor and has three daughters and eight grandchildren, all of whom have contributed to her understanding of women in changing times.

CPSIA information can be obtained
at www.ICGtesting.com
Printed in the USA
LVHW101540181122
733278LV00018B/899

9 781684 982684